In his new book, *Th*
captures the essence
practice owner need
is written makes for an easy read. It also manages to
relatively complex subject matter into short, easy to understand
lessons. The information presented in this book will save new
practice owners tens of thousands of dollars. As a practice
owner in a scratch start up, I had to learn many of these lessons
the Hard way. I wish that this book had existed then! My only
disagreement with Dr. Campbell is that what he is teaching
needs to be shouted from the rooftops not whispered about!

Christopher "Doc" Hoffpauir DDS
Founder of The Business of Dentistry
Co-Owner of DentalHub360.com

Dr. Travis Campbell is a young dentist phenom! He "gets it!"
In a relatively short career span, Dr. Campbell has quickly
become an industry thought leader. His experience, insight and
continued zest for learning have led to his new book release, *The
Practice Whisperer*, a compendium of boots-on-the-ground rules
of the road for any dentist who desires to increase bottom-line
profits while decreasing stress and burnout. He dispels many
of the myths and misinformation of dental practice today and
shows the reader how to navigate the complexities of being an
exceptional dentist, business owner, and leader while still having
a life outside of work. Every dentist (and dentist office) should
have this book as a primary guide and resource!

Dr. David Phelps
Freedom Founders

# The Practice Whisperer

Practical Steps to Achieving
Growth & Increasing Profit
While Reducing Stress

Dr. Travis Campbell

Clovercroft Publishing

The Practice Whisperer: Practical Steps to Decreasing Stress and Increasing Profit in Your Dental Practice

©2019 by Travis Campbell

Published by Clovercroft Publishing, Franklin, Tennessee

Senior Editor: Tammy Kling

Executive Editor: Tiarra Tompkins

Copy Edit by Adept Content Solutions

Cover Design by Nelly Sanchez

Interior Design by Adept Content Solutions

Printed in the United States of America

ISBN:   978-1-948484-67-1

# Contents

# Acknowledgments

I never started out intending to write a book; the process seemed so daunting. It was far more involved than I ever imagined it would be. However, the challenge has been rewarding and it is impressive to see how many people are involved with the process.

Most importantly, I want to thank my wonderful wife, Susan. You gave me the space and time needed to invest in making this book a reality. The love and support you have given over the last 10 years are phenomenal.

Special thanks to my mother, who spent almost as much time proofreading this book as my editor. Her years of expertise with human resource management also helped shape the content in sections. I am eternally grateful for being your son.

To my editor, Tiarra, thank you for all your help and guidance. You never complained about the phone calls at odd hours or the random questions. I would never have made it through this process without your expertise and coaching.

Thank you to Larry, Nelly, Lori, and the rest of the edit and publishing team for all your work pulling all the pieces together. Especially thank you for the crunch times and rapid turnaround when it was needed. I never realized how much work was involved with getting a book from manuscript to print.

None of this, of course, would have been possible without my exceptional office team! I am most appreciative of all your great work, the inspiration you provide, as well as the occasional kick in the rear when needed. You have been instrumental in our office success, working through all the changes we have made over the years to get where we are now. Much of what I have learned is from my time with you.

The friends I have made in dentistry are a blessing and have helped me with edits and support. Thank you, Dr. Chris Hoffpauir and Dr. Glenn Vo, for all the great conversations we have had, your friendship means a lot. Both of you are a testament to what dentists should be do as a group to help each other. Dr. David Phelps thank you for driving me to finish this book far earlier than I ever intended. Thank you, Frank Curtin, for some great insight, support, and friendship. And to all the dentists out there who pushed me to write a book in the first place, thank you!

There are so many people who touch our lives in various ways that it is impossible to acknowledge them all. Thank you to everyone who gives of themselves to help others grow their talents. The more we build each other up, the better our society becomes.

# Introduction

Do you ever feel practicing dentistry is the easy part of your day, while running the business is what always causes problems? Have you reached a plateau in the business you just cannot get over? Have you ever wondered why marketing isn't as successful as you thought it should be? Perhaps you are concerned about difficult team members, patients, or unemployment issues are driving you crazy? Maybe you have lost some of your enthusiasm for the office and coming to work just feels like a job? I have been there!

If you're like many dentists, you're used to simple answers because most of dentistry is visual, direct, and easy to diagnose. Alternatively, running a business is not what we were trained to do. Business management isn't hard, but it can be complex and requires most of us to think in ways in which we never were trained. The answers are rarely direct. This is why so many of us can get frustrated with trying to fix a problem and not seeing the results we want.

Offices need diagnosis and treatment planning just as much as if not more so than our patients!

I have spent years in online platforms helping other dentists with their day-to-day concerns; I find it very rewarding and fun. I enjoy the puzzle and know how to solve problems. In the last year, I got requests for help or advice from friends, colleagues, and mentees almost daily. I hosted several seminars and even recorded a few for online use. I found I was answering the same questions often, and I knew I could help more by writing it all down. I am writing this book for all those seeking guidance—those who are frustrated with challenges they aren't sure how to fix and who want to improve their businesses and lives in dentistry

Like most dentists, I love what I get to do clinically to help patients every day; however, I also really enjoy the business side of things. That was not always the case. I did not understand from the beginning that being a dentist owner really comes part and parcel with running a business. It is said that the generation before us could really focus on being a dentist, but that is not the case anymore, as insurance and more corporations enter the dental industry and more dentists enter an already saturated market. Today, to compete in the dental industry means knowing how to run a successful business as much as knowing the clinical aspects of being a successful practitioner.

Every office can and should be successful, and success can come in many different forms. A good friend of mine lives in another state and has an office that barely collects above a million a year. He has a different patient demographic, different insurance networks, and diagnoses differently than I do. However, he works three days a week, takes off two months a year, and has a 50 percent profit margin. I think most of us would consider him highly successful even though he collects about half what I do in a year. In many ways, our offices look very different. The one commonality between our offices is the systems, structure, and culture in both of our offices is about the same. The important thing to remember is that there are multiple pathways to success. While dental offices may have different treatment philosophies, insurance participation, and patient groups, the way business runs is not much different in successful practices.

An important facet of success in this industry is to have a strongly-defined vision of how you would like to run your practice and build a sound infrastructure to support that vision. Can you picture it? Can you identify any potential stumbling blocks to achieving that goal? My goal now is to help you home in on that vision and consider it through the lens of tried-and-tested guidelines you may have not considered in order to avoid any unnecessary pitfalls on your road to success.

This book is a story of how I went from knowing nothing to being in the top 1 percent of single-doctor practices in the country. And I want to teach you what I have learned along the way.

I started a practice from scratch and I am well known for telling people that I pretty much made every possible mistake running an office; however, I learned how to fix all the mistakes and avoid them in the future. I have spent a fortune on dental consultants and have learned many lessons through trial and error. My goal is for you is to understand how problems can occur, how to avoid them or fix them, and be able to be successful without all the stress and failures that I have overcome in the past and that many dentists continue to face every day.

Does that sound like the kind of advice that could help you and your practice? Let's get started.

# Chapter 1
# The Journey

I graduated from Baylor College of Dentistry (BCD) in 2009. BCD has since changed names, but it will always be Baylor to me. I was newly married to a wonderful woman, Susan. The year we got married was about the same time I started working on a business plan for my office. I believe I received an amazing clinical education at BCD, but like most dental schools, our education in business was almost non-existent. Our single business class in dental school consisted of a one-hour-a-week seminar that was only minimally useful. About the only thing I can say I got out of that seminar was the drive to write the business plan that I eventually did use for my office. I knew from the start I would not be happy working for someone else for long, and at the time I believed I had a clear view of the office I wanted. I was naïve and had never run a business, but I had the confidence and drive to go for what I wanted.

While most of my classmates were stressing over boards and the Western Regional Examining Board (WREB), I was meeting with suppliers, CPAs, and real estate agents. Once I graduated, I had a full plan in place and everything started with loans and construction. My start-up office opened in October and I believed I was doing fantastic. Oh, how little I knew….

For those who have opened an office from scratch for the first time, you may see a lot of similarities coming up.

I'm not sure how it was for you, but I initially hired an office manager and an assistant, and everything was coming together nicely. Both came with years of experience and seemed to know what was needed without my help—which was great because I did not know what I did not know at the time.

My loan was with Bank of America and they had a new dentist tracking program they call Heartbeat. Basically, this program is to help you keep track of your progress and the general health of your business. It offers advice on problems and guides dentists in their first year. The bank's concept is a good one because it helps them protect their investment by making sure the dentist is going to succeed. The program was required for the first twelve months of being open. I was told at month five that they were suspending the program because I had already surpassed the twelve-month goal they had in place and they no longer needed to track me. As you can imagine, I was very excited; I must have been doing something right!

Looking back, I can tell you I was doing some things well. First, I set up the office mostly correctly, in that I knew my vision and where I ultimately wanted to go. Second, I was also spending a good amount on marketing, which helped a ton as well (as you will see in Chapter 6). Third, I believe I had a natural ability to guide patients through problems to see their ultimate goals. I will go a lot more in detail about this in Chapter 14: Treatment Acceptance.

Lastly, I did understand one huge part of the business—filling a niche and doing something others aren't. For me, that was to be open Fridays and Saturdays. I would highly recommend this strategy for any practice looking for growth. It gave me great initial growth because when most offices were closed Friday and almost all offices are closed Saturday, I was available for emergencies and for patients with busy work schedules. I also rotated days from 7 a.m.–4 p.m. and 9 a.m.–6 p.m. to help patients work around their workweek schedules. On a personal level, having Monday off allowed me a normal-length weekend where I could get a lot more done as well. Almost every other business is open on Monday and everyone else is working, so getting errands done is much easier.

Everything I did wrong? Well, that is what the rest of this book is about.

# Chapter 2
# Overhead—Variable vs. Fixed Expenses

O ne of the first things I learned about dentistry, as a business, is why dentistry is still potentially one of the most profitable businesses to run. This principle concept is that of overhead, which is comprised of variable and fixed expenses.

Fixed expenses do not change based on how many patients you treat. These are also the largest expenses in an office, often accounting for more than three-quarters of your monthly overhead. These expenses include rent, utilities, payroll, marketing, etc.

Variable expenses change based on how much work you do or the patients you treat. Variable expenses include supplies and lab costs, which means they are variable by month depending on how many patients you treat. Variable expenses usually consist of only one quarter of your overhead.

So why are these concepts so important to know about? When you treat more patients, your variable expenses keep going up. As a dentist, you will never get away from spending money on supplies and lab work. You can potentially reduce variable expenses, find less expensive labs, use less expensive supplies, and even find cheaper suppliers, but you will always need more to treat more patients. The common mistake here is focusing so much on cutting small overhead costs that you can easily lose sight of greater benefits and opportunities—stepping over dollars to pick up the pennies.

Fixed expenses are where the focus should be, as understanding these provides the greatest opportunity to impact profitability. If it takes you X amount of money in fixed expenses to treat 100 patients, it also takes you X amount to treat 200 patients. Yet you are going to bring home more profit in treating patient 101-200 vs. the first 100. I apologize to those who don't like numbers; most of this book is about concepts and not math. However, overhead is so important to running a business that I hope you give yourself a chance to get through this numerical section.

See where your office fits in with these examples:

Office A and office B have the same-sized team, one dentist, similar areas, and the same fixed expenses.

Office A produces $100k per month and has the normal 60 percent overhead expense, $45k from fixed expenses and $15k from variable. This leaves office A with $40k profit.

Office B produces $140k per month, pays the same rent, has the same payroll costs, utilities, etc. However, office B also has a 40 percent higher variable expense from doing 40 percent more work ($21k). Office B, therefore, ends up with $74k profit (140k income - 45k fixed - 21k variable), which is almost double the profit of office A, while doing only 40 percent more work.

|  | Office A | Office B |
| --- | --- | --- |
| Production | $100,000 | $140,000 |
| Fixed Expenses | $45,000 | $45,000 |
| Variable Expenses | $15,000 | $21,000 |
| Profit | $40,000 | $74,000 |

This is the efficiency that is fairly unique in dentistry, which is the foundation of why profitability can be so much higher in our industry compared to most others. In most other industries, the variable expenses comprise a much larger chunk of the overhead. Think of a restaurant, one of the least profitable businesses in existence. While dentists average 30-40 percent profit, restaurants average around 5 percent. Why? Their variable expenses (e.g. food and beverages, for example, which have a set shelf life and need constant replenishing) far outweigh their fixed expenses. This means inefficient restaurants fail (90 percent in the first year), efficient ones only barely succeed, and highly efficient ones do only slightly better than the average successful ones.

Variable vs. fixed expenses are critical concepts to master and remember. Not only will I refer back to it often, but it is also the foundation of how you need to think about overhead and profit in your own office.

# Chapter 3
# Office Vision

Any successful business needs a vision and a goal because without these, there really is no way to set up a good, long-term plan for success. There is no limit to the success you can attain when it is built on a strongly-rooted foundation. There are several aspects to an office that distinguish how they should look and function. I want you to consider these options carefully. The choices you make here will have a major impact on how your office is run and, ultimately, how much profit you will make.

## Insurance Participation

I could write an entire book on just the ins and outs of insurance. There are so many aspects that dentists don't know how to navigate well within the world of insurance. I am going to limit this to a single chapter, though, and just hit the main highlights. If you are interested in more detailed specifics about insurance rules, how to handle insurance coding, and how to become highly successful with dental insurance, please find my online continuing education (CE) at PracticeWhisper.com.

**Fee-For-Service offices:** FFS means you collect full fee from the patient and the patient waits on their insurance company to issue repayment to them. These offices should never have collection problems because they get paid up front, and treatment plans are completely accurate because they don't rely on insurance estimates.

**Out-Of-Network offices:** Often confused with FFS, OON offices have not signed any contracts, but agree to wait on the portion of the fees the insurance company will pay rather than collect upfront from the patient. Due to getting full fees as with FFS, these offices can succeed with fewer patients. However, the segment of the population that is willing to pay more is a lot smaller, and they are usually looking for more than just an average dentist. To succeed in an FFS or OON, the dentist needs to be an amazing leader, communicator, and motivator, as well as an excellent clinician. They need to stand out from the majority of other dentists in their area.

**In-Network offices:** These offices have agreed to accept discounted fees, wait for insurance checks, and follow a host of other rules the insurance company sets. Due to the discounted rates, these offices need efficiency and lots of patients to succeed.

Here is the math you need to understand about participating in any kind of discount. Most dental offices run about 60 percent overhead, meaning 40 percent profit (ADA averages).

So, if you cut your fees by 20 percent, you cut profit in half and you have to do twice as much work to see the same amount of profit. Do you see how much of a difference that makes? How would a 20 percent reduction in fees affect your business? How many additional patients would you need to see to compensate for lost profit?

If you cut your fees by 30 percent, you have to do four times as much work to earn the same profit. That's huge!

Most insurance discounts are between 30–50 percent from the average fee.

Can you see why being in-network and accepting lower fees means an office has to be extremely efficient to survive, much less succeed?

In summary with insurance participation, FFS offices tend to have the least number of patients with the highest profit per patient, while the in-network offices tend to need the greatest number of patients and work with the lowest profit per patient. Now, I am not suggesting you cannot succeed being in-network. Currently, as I write this book, I still have about 70 percent in-network patients. However, while an FFS or OON office can work with some inefficiency, being in-network means success only comes with highly efficient systems in place and surpassing their fixed expenses (Chapter 2).

## Office Size

Next, you want to decide how large you want the office to be. Do you want a slow-paced two-operatory office with one doctor or do you want a large, fast-paced office with ten chairs and multiple doctors?

Personally, I decided I wanted something in between.

The size of the office helps you decide how many employees you need, what your budgets are going to be, and how much marketing you need. All of these will help you figure out how much money you need to collect each month to start making a profit and, therefore, what goals you need to set to reach that point. Vision and goals need to be clearly defined to set a strong foundational infrastructure!

## Associates

Along with size comes the number of doctors you want working in the office eventually. For example, a two-operatory office is only ever going to work for one doctor, while a seven-op office is eventually going to need at least two or three to cover the cost of the size.

A single-doctor office is by far the simplest to run because you only have to handle one treatment philosophy, and there is a single source for dental information. However, you tend to have to work more often and have less flexibility with being able to get away from the office for CE or vacation.

In contrast, bringing in one or more associates may be more complex to handle, with multiple providers, each with their own personalities and philosophies. In exchange, you get more flexibility with the doctors' schedules, their ability to take vacation, ability to avoid being called in for emergencies, and have a better ability to utilize the equipment and space in the office to offset the fixed costs of rent and equipment.

## Procedure Mix

What procedures do you want to offer in the office? Your choice of procedures can have a wide range of effects such as the types of skill sets for which you need to train; equipment and supplies you purchase; how you market the office; as well as which demographic of patients you treat and what you talk to them about in the office.

## Price

There is a common adage with all businesses called the Unattainable Triangle. In a restaurant, you can have something fast, cheap, or good but you can never have all three at once. Think of McDonald's, they choose to have it fast and cheap, but the quality is what suffers. In dentistry, those terms become price, service, and quality. In order to provide the lowest price, you cannot also provide the best service and best quality at the same time.

So what mix of the three do you want to focus on? Which align with the type of office you want to run? Which would your existing clients prefer? Or your target clients?

To be in-network, you are now choosing to offer the lowest price, so you need to decide: are you going to sacrifice quality or service? To be FFS at a higher price, you need to know that patients will expect a higher level of quality and service.

Now, please don't mistake these concepts. Yes, in dentistry we are held to a minimum standard of quality by state boards and ethics, but there is a wide range above that minimum. When ordering a crown from a lab, for example, you can get one for anywhere from $69 to $500, all of which can be minimally acceptable quality. With service, you can have hygienists who are highly motivated to spend time educating patients on their dental health and home care, or you can have hygienists who are silent prophy machines. As the dentist, you can focus on efficiency and be able to prep a crown in five minutes, or you can focus on quality and spend thirty minutes making sure each prep is worthy of publishing in JADA (Journal of the American Dental Association). Every office is unique in where they fall along this triangle, but knowing where you want to be can help you plan the office and make those difficult decisions later.

Let's work on an example and create the Unattainable Triangle for your office.

Pull out a sheet of paper and draw a large triangle. Now label each side as the following categories: "lowest price," "highest quality," and "best service." Each side can have a value up to 10 in how much focus you put into that category.

Now allocate values to each side up to a total of 20 keeping in mind the vision for your office. Place a dot inside the triangle that visually represents the values you provided to each side. This triangle now represents the focus of your practice. Now keep that triangle in your office or somewhere close by and always refer to it when making decisions about the office so you can stick to your vision.

A great resource to go to about price is www.fairhealthconsumer.org. This website will give you the average price in your zip code for any dental procedure. You do need to be aware of how price percentiles work to understand it fully.

Offices under the fiftieth percentile focus on price first and foremost. These tend to be low-income clinics or other government-subsidized offices. Private practices are almost exclusively above the fiftieth percentile, which makes their average price for an area in the seventy-fifth percentile.

## Office Vision Overview

Pulling all these concepts together is what helps make each individual office somewhat unique and allows great flexibility in how you can achieve success as a dentist in different types of scenarios. Understanding each of these concepts and how they change the look and feel of an office can help you plan your business model, goals, and journey.

To get back to the story, I will tell you I eventually wanted several things:

- Strong Profitability

- Flexibility in the schedule when I have children (associates)

- Someplace I could be proud of my work without spending a fortune (quality)

- Someplace my patients would love to come (service)
- Where patients could get a majority of procedures done (convenience)
- All in an office that was not too much headache to run (single location, moderate size)

Think about what you want with your office. And think precisely. If you set clear, exact goals and expectations for your office, it will give you a clear path forward.

Setting these goals led me to design my office around an eventual eight-op office, with two to three general dentist associates, focusing on good quality/great service/average price, with a couple of specialists coming to the office as needed, in a single facility. Now, of course, starting from scratch means it would be crazy to try to get all this at once. And here is where I encountered my first major failure—not planning for the process and not understanding how insurance fits into it all.

My first office was five ops, moderate appearance, minimal service (because I did not know what was really needed), and low initial profit (because I did not have good systems in place).

If I had to do this over or was making suggestions to a new dentist who wanted to open from scratch, here is the scenario I would recommend. First, it would be evaluating whether a scratch start is a good idea. There are a variety of reasons why. The most important reason is location and competition. If you want to open in a rural area that needs a dentist, starting from scratch is great. If you want to be in the middle of Dallas-Fort Worth with 100 dentists in a ten-block radius, a start-up is a horrible idea. There are also a variety of financial reasons why starting from scratch ends up costing you more. Going into those is a large discussion that would take me off track. I welcome you to email or message me if you would like to know more details.

However, since this book is about my office, which I did open from scratch:

- Have your ideal office goals in mind first (vision)
- Plan your size based on this vision.
- Buy inexpensive equipment and decorations that look decent but don't cost much.
- Build your patient pool with low expenses and pay off those initial loans fast
- Utilize the office to its fullest space capacity
- And then use your profits to expand size, equipment, or locations.

Create your vision and set up a strong set of systems to run the office. Whether this is from doing it yourself or hiring a coach, doing it wrong can cost you far more than just paying to get help to do it right from the start.

# Chapter 4
# Hygienists

O ne of the most common questions I get regularly is "When should I hire my first hygienist?" This story should help illustrate some of the things to look for considering this step.

My first few months went really well. By month four I had a couple hundred patients had already started making a profit, and was seeing good growth in the schedule and collections. I was open three days a week, my office manager answered the phones five days a week, and my assistant worked with me when I was there. I worked part-time at another office while I was growing to make sure I had an income level where I did not have to worry about personal expenses. My schedule was full out about one week consistently. I hired one hygienist for one day a week (Sarah) and she brought a colleague (Kelly) a few weeks later, who started as well, because Sarah did not want to work Saturdays.

These two hygienists are still with me today and have taught me a ton about how hygienists should look and act in a dental office. They are one of the main reasons for my early success that I did not even appreciate until years later when I really started researching the *why* of success.

## Education

First, let's look at our education and be honest with ourselves. Dental school is four years and focused on everything from prevention to extractions. There is so much we need to know that our focus on any one topic is limited. Business was likely the least taught portion; however, I would say hygiene and periodontal disease (perio) were likely number two (at least at Baylor). Yes, we were taught how to recognize severe perio and how surgery works, but somewhere I think we missed details and experience in the diagnosis of day-to-day cases.

In contrast, hygienists spend two years focusing on one aspect only: hygiene and periodontal disease. While we have to do hundreds of restorations, they have to diagnose and treat hundreds of different patients from healthy to severe perio. Most hygienists are likely better at perio charting and co-diagnosis of gum health than most dentists. How can they not be when they spend their whole education on one thing and do it every day thereafter?

The amount I learned from the hygienists of a combined 50 years' experience, was immense, and it was confirmed by everything I have seen and learned since.

The most noticeable thing I found about myself was that I really did not care much about perio because cleaning calculus just seemed boring to me compared to fixing broken teeth. A good friend told me once, "I did not become a dentist to be a gum gardener." This led to the fact that I was pretty light with periodontal charting because I just wanted to be finished with it so we could talk about the pearly white things in the mouth. I also did not want to hurt the patient. Periodontal charting with minimal to no pain is an art that takes skill and repetition. Once I actually learned to probe with correct amounts of pressure, the periodontal chart and the X-rays actually started to match better.

A common problem in dentistry is X-rays (which show bone loss) and perio charting (measurements) that don't match up. Corporate offices tend to push where the measurements are way above what the X-rays show. Many private or older offices have X-rays with severe damage and charting that looks normal.

In either case, the data does not match, which in healthcare often means something is being done wrong.

So how would you know for yourself? Look at the data.

The ADA has studies showing 70 percent of patients in America have some form of periodontal disease. The AAP says 80 percent. This can be a range, but it basically means that these patients may or may not need scaling and root planning, but all need something more than a prophylaxis every six months.

Now also bring in the studies showing that 50 percent of Americans never visit the dentist. Let's take the most conservative approach and say *all* of those patients have some form of periodontal disease. That leaves you with 40–60 percent of the patients that come to see you (the remaining 20–30 percent) that have some form of periodontal disease and need something more than six-month prophylaxis. Now when you look at insurance tables and see that over 85 percent of patients get only six-month cleanings, you can see where something overall is missing in the equation. Knowing the data can help you evaluate if you are seeing and treating what you need, or if you and your hygienists are missing something. Think about your office. Are you examining the data? Are you treating everything you could be treating? Are you giving your patients the best dental care you can provide?

## Loss Leaders

The first reason I hear any dentist say to not get a hygienist early is because they are expensive.

Technically that is true because other than another dentist, your hygienists will be your highest paid team members. A loss leader is a product or service that is sold at a loss to attract a customer. Too many dentists see hygiene as a loss leader because they aren't looking at the math and they don't respect the Unattainable Triangle.

So first, let's look at the Triangle again. The three sides are:

- Lowest price (such as in-network prices)
- Highest quality (skill, education, preventive aids)
- Highest service (in this case, time)

You cannot have all three at the same time, but that does not mean you have to lose money. As an example, here is a doctor I worked with in the Dallas-Fort Worth area who was having concerns about hygiene losses.

Dr. Smith has an office with a hygienist who has been there for twenty years. The hygienist is given sixty minutes with each patient regardless of what the patient needs or is scheduled to do. Dr. Smith has been in-network for years and did not feel like he could get out. He had heard about the goal of getting hygienists to produce three times their salary but could not think how to reach that point. When we investigated the numbers, it was pretty clear what the problem was. The hygienist makes a well-above-average $45 per hour, and the insurance company paid on average $90 per visit, and $50 on a cleaning only. The average room turnover and supply costs, according to the ADA, are $25.

So, for cleaning only visits the hygienist costs $45 + $25 for the hour, and the doctor got paid $50 for an immediate loss of $20. For other visits at $90, he was not making much. Taking into consideration the overhead for the office, this was costing him a lot of money.

How does this work in your office? Is the hygienist always profitable? If not, can you diagnose the problem so you can correct it?

Overall, Dr. Smith's hygiene department was a loss leader. With help, it only took him a month to change that and become profitable. We focused on the triangle and changed the situation to what worked best for him. This works differently for different offices based on what your goals are, so let's look at each section.

## Time

If you break down each part of the visit by procedure or task you can really get a good idea about how to schedule different appointments. Ask most experienced hygienists and they will tell you a prophy on a healthy adult takes about twenty to thirty minutes and ten to fifteen minutes on a child. Taking digital X-rays should take five minutes. A routine exam takes ten minutes including the doctor time. Talking to the patient and reviewing medical history should take five to ten minutes. If you do everything (exam/X-rays/prophy) sixty minutes makes sense given a ten-minute cleanup and setup time for an adult patient. However, when you are not doing an exam and X-rays, or when you are seeing a child, that same hygienist does not need sixty minutes for the visit. Cutting those visits down to thirty to forty minutes can make things a lot more realistic and turn them from loss leader to profit center. Remember, a vast majority of your expense in the hygiene department is time.

A common complaint I hear from other dentists from their hygienists is that patients "just need more time." The most common reason for this is a misdiagnosed patient. The hygienist is trying to fight periodontal problems but is not being given the time to do it. Some patients also just build up calculus faster and therefore need to be seen more often than every six months. Ortho patients tend to have a harder time with plaque and calculus buildup and need to be seen more frequently. Pregnant patients often develop pregnancy gingivitis and need more frequent care.

Lastly, there are patients who just will not stop talking, even with a running handpiece in their mouth. I am sure you have probably seen some of these in your office. Mrs. Jones, a 70 y/o widow who uses her doctor visits as a social event, is a common patient like this.

These patients always remind me of my three-year-old daughter, who does not stop talking from the moment she wakes up until she starts snoring at night. It is extremely cute, but not conducive to doing anything quickly. Eating can take an hour because every bite is separated by constant questions. Does she really need an hour to eat? Nope. So, when we have a time crunch (like a hygiene visit) we tell her what that time is, and she only gets to eat as much as she can during the time she has. The more she talks, the less food she gets to eat. It's all her choice.

The same goes with the patient. The hygienist has a set time to see them, and the patient is welcome to fill that time however they want: talking OR cleaning. Guess what happens when you set that standard that the procedure is X time and that is all you get? The hygienist will tend to work quicker, and the patient will learn to talk less during the procedure. Let the hygienist talk to the patient some BEFORE or AFTER the visit, while your assistant is helping her clean the room and set up for the next one.

Think of it this way: each service you provide comes with a set time and cost. There are many ways to handle patients who "just need more time" without actually spending more chair time.

Do you have patients who love to talk, who take up a lot of your and your employees' time? Most offices do. Perhaps you can think of other ways to manage them. The trick is to let them feel that they're important to you whilst gently letting them know that your time together is limited.

## Quality of Care

An alternative or adjunctive option to changing time is to provide the patient with more quality of care options. We all know fluoride and sealants are good for any patient and especially for moderate-to-high risk patients. When you increase the quality of education you provide a patient, you will naturally notice that they will accept more dental care: everything from perio treatment to fluoride to anything else a hygienist can legally do. Give the hygienist the training she needs to educate patients about these things and the freedom to do so. This will not only increase the level of quality you provide to the patient, but will also increase the price you receive for that visit.

If you are in an office that has 85 percent or more of the patients on six-month visits, are you really getting an abnormal number of healthy patients? Or are you missing something? One extra Scaling and Root Planing (SRP) a day can almost double a hygienist's production.

Regardless of what you decide is worthwhile to you for the patient, offering a higher level of care and prevention helps both the patient and the office.

## Price

If neither of those options works for you, there are two last resorts—either shred that network contract to increase the price of care or hire a less expensive hygienist and decrease the expense to provide that care.

The range of pay that hygienists will get in any area is amazing. It varies significantly around the country, but the ranges tend to be the same. For the sake of simplicity, I will talk about the ranges in the Dallas-Fort Worth area. Hygienists here make on average between $30 and $45/hour, with some outliers as high as $55. If you have that $55/hour hygienist, you can bet that office is not running PPOs and is likely a periodontist. Therefore, the hygienist can still be paid $55/hour and bring in more than three times her salary. If you try to take that same hygienist and put them in a PPO office that collects $50 per cleaning, this is what creates loss leaders.

The next thing to think about is what the hygienists themselves are worth. Anyone can clean teeth; the real difference in what makes a great hygienist is how quickly they can connect with a patient. It is a skill that can be honed over the years, but experience alone does not mean you learned it. Experience should not be the reason any hygienist earns more money. People and communication skills mean far more. Kelly and Sarah, my two main hygienists, both have great people skills, and most patients fall in love with them instantly. They also have experience working with patients who have periodontal disease and know how to communicate a fairly hidden and complex problem on a level the patient can easily understand. They have a consistent, over 95 percent acceptance rate on getting patients to understand the problem and accept treatment. Without those skills, neither would be worth what they get paid.

So, if you have a long-term team but are struggling with low profit margins like Dr. Smith, you might first want to see if you have a hygienist who is getting paid more than she is worth. Think about this—providers are "worth" more when they can accomplish more in the same amount of time. Dentists who can do more quality work per hour earn more. If you have a hygienist who is really worth more, she can get things done without needing more time. How is a hygienist who constantly runs over time or cannot seem to get things done worth more? If she is accepting of change, there is potential to turn her into an amazing hygienist. If not, it may be time to replace her.

## Overall

Whichever option you choose, the math just needs to make sense. And often, whichever you choose depends on the type of office you have a vision of creating. Since it is impossible to provide the highest level of quality and service and the lowest price, making a decision about where you want to go is paramount to success.

Dr. Smith's hygienist was near retirement and was unwilling to change. He hired a new hygienist who was upbeat with a great attitude and who was able to provide the same service in less time and was paid $8 less per hour. The new hygienist also came with a desire to provide more adjunctive care to patients (like Fluoride). Overall, Dr. Smith was able to more appropriately schedule his hygiene appointments, paid less for his hygienist, and provided the patient with better care that was compensated. We were able to quickly change his loss leader hygiene department into a profit center that also treated the patient better. Patients commented daily on how much they liked the new, positive atmosphere the new hygienist brought.

I can tell you that for my office, with hygiene, I went with high quality. The better education helped me stay in-network but also maintain a moderate price. However, we also change the length of appointments based on what we are doing. Child patients are blocked for forty minutes, as are adults that are not due for exam and X-rays. New patient adults, however, get ninety minutes because we know that to diagnose everything correctly, we need to have time to discuss things like lots of treatment or periodontal disease; also, a prophy or starting an SRP takes more than a sixty-minute appointment.

Be willing to be flexible to account for the needs of your patients, while also considering the health of your practice as well.

## New Patients

How long do you give your new patients? I get the question a lot: "Why 90 minutes?" It can seem counterintuitive when talking about decreasing the time spent on every other hygiene visit. One thing to think about is the statistics that many GP offices have a low acceptance for cases worth $5,000 or more compared to specialist offices. Most of that is just how we treat patients. How many patients are going to walk in, meet you the first time for a ten-minute exam, and be willing to give you a ton of money that day? That is likely a hard pill for anyone to swallow.

I had a new patient (NP) come in one week through hygiene, who needed a lot of dental work. She had no periodontal concerns, so the hygienist only needed half the ninety minutes with her. I spent the other forty-five minutes talking to her, developing a relationship, and discussing her treatment needs and options. She prepaid her $10,000 treatment before she left. That was not likely to happen if I zipped in and out in ten minutes because the appointment was only booked for an hour. When you treat your new patients like gold and genuinely show you care about them, it will pay off.

Now, if you are one of the doctors who likes to see the patients first, great. That process can work just as well. Success comes down to how you connect with the patient. Sometimes the doctor is better at that; other times, the hygienist is. The key to acceptance on hygiene treatment is education and tying any needs to the patient's desires and story, so being a very good listener and communicator goes a long way. Whoever is better at connecting with people should be the first one the patient sees.

Who is best at dealing with patients and building relationships in your office? Are they the ones who actually spend the most time interacting with the patients? Who is setting the expectation or precedent for care?

Doctor-run NP appointments are nice for one hour. Hygiene-run NP appointments are best for ninety minutes because the patient has the expectation of getting their teeth cleaned as well.

Regardless of who sees the patient first, a full perio chart is key to hygiene success. PSR is a waste of time, and the boards don't accept them anyway. AAP states patients must have a full periodontal charting at least once per year. Without it, you will end up missing a lot of periodontal problems that you could have caught early.

This both increases production and is a better service for the patient's oral health. Plus, I get shocked looks from patients almost weekly when we go through the whole process. So many offices will glaze over periodontal charting, and patients can tell the difference. Having a patient ask you why their previous dentist was not so thorough is a great opportunity to shine. It is just another "wow" factor setting you apart in that first visit. Would doing something that impresses your patients like this have an impact on your office?

My hygienists see most of our new patients first. If the hygienist sees the patient, realize the patient has the expectation of getting a cleaning the same day. Since we are in the business of taking care of patients, it is important to work with that idea in mind. I have noticed that SRP same day goes a long way towards treatment acceptance, and there is no reason you should not be able to do at least one or two quads in a ninety-minute appointment. We have had a 95 percent acceptance rate with periodontal treatment when we are available to start the process that day.

When you notice the patient needs periodontal treatment, focus just on the perio. You can put a preliminary plan together and do an extremely quick review for the patient of their overall oral health, but focus on the perio only so that you can use that time for same-day treatment. You are going to want to see that patient back in four to six weeks anyway, which is the perfect time to discuss the rest of their treatment needs. This also helps avoid overwhelming the patient with too much information on their first visit.

Now, what about the patient who has no periodontal issues? Many of them may have a lot of treatment needs. With ninety minutes, you have time to discuss those in detail, answer any patient concerns, and get them on your schedule to start taking care of them.

And finally, with the new patient who has no periodontal issues and has minimal or no treatment needs, you can still use that extra time well. Take your time and show them they are the most important person in your office at that moment. You and your hygienist have a great opportunity to develop a relationship with that patient that will keep them coming back for years.

Having a great hygienist is highly important to all of this. However, a great hygienist will do poorly with a poor system, and a mediocre hygienist can do well with a great system. Having a system and goals in place is part of being a good leader. Everything from how the hygienist relays information to the doctor, to them all knowing how the doctor diagnoses treatment means everything. The patient sees, hears, and evaluates everything. New patients have only a first visit impression of you to make a decision on whether to come back or not. A good team flow between all members of the team speaks volumes to the patient.

How does this work in your office? Think about the "patient journey." How is their experience from booking an appointment to getting the treatment? Looking at things from the patient's perspective will help you give them the best experience possible.

## How to Get There

If you are starting a practice from scratch, then you can easily put this entire plan together before you open the office and therefore never have to deal with change. The rest of us that started with hygienists who are used to their old ways and are resistant to change may need some additional help. (I will address this in a later chapter in how to motivate people to change and grow with the office.) Regardless of how you want to handle the Unattainable Triangle, any office can get to the point of hygiene profitability. The greatest part is that hygiene is the part of the office that makes money without the dentist having to do more work. The most successful dentists are the ones who are able to leverage the work of others as well as their own.

# Chapter 5
# Marketing

How much marketing do you do? What kind of marketing? Do you think marketing is important?

I'm often asked what I would do differently at the beginning of my start-up office if I had to do it all over again. The number one thing that would make the largest difference by far is marketing more. As a general business rule, your marketing budget should be set based on your goals and what you plan to collect.

There are four main tiers of marketing:

1. Decline—Spending nothing often leads to a decline in patient population and income. This is because patients will often move away, pass away, or decide to see another dentist. Attrition is a natural part of any business. Offices where the dentist is giving up or near retirement tend to be here, as well as offices that just don't understand the nature of business.

2. Maintenance— The average dental office, according to the ADA, needs about twenty-five new patients per month to grow at all. In order to maintain the size of the office,

27

most offices will need somewhere near that number to counteract the attrition. A good range for cost is 1–3 percent of your monthly collections to spend. This is often where most mature practices end up once their schedule is completely full and they don't want to change anything else.

3. Slow growth—Usually 4–7 percent will get you enough patients to grow slowly. Many offices stop here and then complain that they are spending money but not seeing the results they want.

4. Fast growth—In order to grow quickly, a business really needs to look at spending 8–10 percent of the income they want to generate. Getting 75–100 new patients or more per month has a cost to it. Every new office and office in active growth mode should be here. Remember, though, that it is a percentage of where you want to be, not where you are currently.

Where does your business fit in these scenarios? Are you doing enough marketing for the growth you want? Like any business, you won't attract new customers if they don't know you exist. Marketing is just a way of showing people who you are and what you can do for them. Be present and let your potential patients know what you have to offer.

## Marketing Cycle

I often hear a lot of concerns from doctors that they are spending a lot of money on marketing but not getting the results they want. In order to understand this, we must first understand the cycle that goes on that takes patients from seeing your ad to spending money. Return on Investment (ROI) is simply a number tracking how good your entire system is in providing results from the marketing money you spend. However, there is more to it than just where you spend the money.

Let's look at an average patient, Sally, in the life of a dental practice and the journey she takes. First, she must have a need for seeing a dentist, which could be anything from needing a hygiene visit to having an emergency. Like many patients, Sally is due for her six-month hygiene visit and is aware of no other dental needs. She sees your marketing ad along with several other dentists and something must appeal to Sally to get her to pick your office over the others. It's likely she has seen your logo or ad in a few other places over time, since most people have to be exposed to something three to seven times before they react.

Sally is then likely to visit your website and also find online reviews that give her a sense of security that you would be a good office to pick.

Finally, Sally calls your office and talks to a team member about making an appointment. If something did not go well in that call, Sally is either not going to schedule or not going to show up for her appointment. The phone call is Sally's first impression and experience with the office. This is why phone skills are so important. Often offices put their least experienced person on the phone, which does not bode well for your ROI.

Sally shows up for her first appointment and has several interactions before she ever meets the dentist. Her first in-person impression of the office has a lot to do with how she is greeted and what experience she has with your paperwork and policies. Is she treated like a guest in a home or like a number in a medical office? Does the assistant or hygienist introduce themselves by name and welcome her? Do they give her a tour of the office and introductions to other team members? Are things explained to her about why your office is different, or do you become just another faceless dental office? All of this goes into her experience and how comfortable she feels about not only staying, but also spending money.

Now she meets the hygienist and/or doctor. Her first experience with the provider means a lot. Sally wants to feel like she is an important person and not just another set of teeth. Does she get the feeling that you care about her as an individual? Sally also wants to see if you can communicate a complex topic of dentistry on a level she can understand. She may NEED some dental work, but she WANTS it to be able to fit into her lifestyle (time and financial). Sally is emotionally driven, like most humans, and uses logic to justify her emotional choices. Sally will not purchase something if she does not FEEL it is something she wants. (This is the problem dentists have, because most of us like appealing to the logical side more than the emotional). Does Sally feel that the team is looking out for her best interests? Does she feel the team understands her enough to match her life to the treatment they say she needs? Does she feel that spending money with this team is the best thing for her?

Sally has taken this entire journey so far, and still has not spent a dime. There are so many places that could be not perfect and therefore send Sally out without accepting treatment. All of this without a discussion of the next step: a treatment plan. Now the plan has to match everything else in Sally's experience for her to accept the plan. Once all these previous steps come together AND the office provides a way for Sally to fit this plan into her financial life is when she gives the office money. Which brings us to the ultimate answer on: ROI because money has now been collected. ROI is partially about how many patients come to the office, but often is more affected by how the office performs once the patient has called that truly matters. Then you also want to think about the free marketing that happens when you have surpassed the patient's expectations: word-of-mouth referrals.

Would you like to improve your ROI? Have you evaluated more than just the marketing you are spending money on? Does your team convert every patient who calls into a happy, paying, long-term member of your patient pool? What would it mean to your office to double your ROI without spending another marketing dollar?

## Where to Spend Marketing Money

Now that we have talked about Sally's journey, we can talk about where to spend money. I often get questions about what marketing company to work with or if one should go with PPC, magazines, mailers, etc.

Sadly, the answer is not just "company X" or "Ad Y." As the journey shows, marketing is a complex cycle that starts with the first impression the office gives (the marketing effort) and ends with the patient coming to the office and accepting some form of treatment. And every step along that path is important to the success of your marketing. Where to spend the money has more to do with the entire cycle than the first step. Ideally you need multiple sources of marketing because patients typically see you several times before deciding they need to do something about it.

So where can you start? Look at the marketing cycle and ask yourself the following questions:

1.  What message is your marketing piece sending and what types of patients does it attract?
2.  Does your website convey the same message and does it commit them to calling?
3.  How effective is your team at getting callers to being scheduled (over 70 percent)?
4.  Do they motivate patients to WANT to come in?
5.  What is the patient's experience when they reach your office and do they accept treatment when they come?

6. Are you rescheduling a vast majority of your patients, or are they getting lost out the back?

7. Is the doctor effective at explaining conditions and getting patients to WANT dental care?

8. Is the doctor/team putting enough urgency in care that the patients feel the importance of getting treatment now?

9. Are you doing great work and patients rarely have a reason to complain?

10. Are you getting good reviews from patients AND getting them to post them online?

How is your business handling the above points? Is there anything you could be doing better or differently to suit your goals?

All of these aspects have far more impact on the success of the marketing effort than which company is printing/posting your content. Great marketing can fail miserably if you aren't getting everything else right because ROI only comes when the potential patient actually spends money with you.

The next time you wonder "How do I get a good ROI?" remember Sally's journey. First evaluate everything else that is happening before you write a check to that marketing company. Answering the questions above can give you a good starting point in that process.

One of the earliest marketing projects I started that I still do is how I handle my business cards. All my cards have my cell phone number on them. My office message machine has my number on it. Every patient I meet is advised to call or text me with concerns or emergencies.

Does it ever get abused? Not yet in nine years. With most people, the first thing out of their mouth when I answer personally is: "I am so sorry to bother you, but...."

Two great things come out of it, though:

1. Patient retention: Many patient concerns are small, but when unaddressed, can lead to major headaches. Talking to the patient directly when the concern comes up helps resolve it quickly and easily.

2. New patient growth: I cannot tell you how many new patients I have gained from this. Most dentists will not even answer their phone after hours, which leads the patient to someone who will. Take good care of an emergency patient, and you gain their loyalty almost instantly. These calls rarely take more than five minutes.

I do not mind driving seven minutes to the office for full-fee care plus $150 after-hours additional fee. Fifty dollars goes to the assistant that comes to help. Most visits are short (<1 hour) and produce anywhere from $500 to $1500. I am sure this won't work for everyone, but if I am in town, I do not mind helping someone in pain and taking home some extra cash as well. And now, who becomes the first person they call with a dental problem in the future? They will call the one who already took care of them in the past. Sometimes it's the small things that have the biggest impact.

# Chapter 6
# Office Managers

About two years into my practice, I was already doing better than the average office. I was marketing heavily due to recommendations, and it was working amazingly well, averaging between 80 and 120 new patients per month. I was collecting over $700k. My hygienists were doing great, and my assistant was also amazing with patients. However, one of my early major mistakes running the office ended up causing a whirlwind of drama.

I had to fire my office manager. Firing her was not the mistake; the office became almost instantly better once she and those who she was connected to were gone. The mistake was when I hired her in the first place. Don't get me wrong; she was a very sweet person who had twenty years of experience in dentistry. The problem came about because I did not understand what an office manager really was or what I really should have been looking for in the first place. I ultimately hired someone with the wrong personality to manage who did not actually have the right experience, and what experience she did have was in a completely different kind of office.

Let's start with the definition itself. A manager or supervisor is someone who supervises people. In every other business on the planet, that means someone who hires, trains, disciplines, and fires employees that they supervise. Generally accepted business practice has a manager oversee between five and twenty employees, with the ideal sweet spot being around six. (This is where I occasionally lose dentists, so put down the book and go Google it if you don't believe me yet.) The title of *office manager* is misused very often in dentistry. Most offices have someone with that title, but often they are just receptionists who are overpaid and overtitled. This leads to increased overhead and often mismanagement and confusion within the team.

Now, let's break down what that means for a dental office.

First is that the average dental office is four to five people, plus the dentist. There just aren't enough people to justify a dedicated manager. Often, this means the dentist is the office manager and does not even know it.

Second, look at the tasks involved in typical management in every industry: hire, train, discipline, and terminate. They also traditionally set goals, handle payroll, track day-to-day performance and trends, and help the owner/CEO stay on track with long-term plans. Notice nowhere listed are their tasks like answering the phones, creating treatment plans, and dealing with insurance.

If you are thinking, "my office manager is awesome, but has different tasks." Great, that means you may have an amazing employee with the wrong job title. As a team, brainstorm what their job description entails, and then give them a title that matches the tasks they are doing.

Lastly, is the average wage or salary. Typically, a manager should make an obvious amount more than the people they are managing. In a dental office, this tends to be somewhere between what assistants/receptionists and hygienists make. Use current local ranges here:

- Assistants / Front Desk: $10–$25 hourly
- Office Managers: $25–$35 hourly
- Hygienists: $32–$45 hourly

## So Where do the problems come in?

The first problem comes in the form of salary and expectations. I cannot count anymore the number of dentists who have asked me what to do because their office manager feels they are not paid enough. I completely understand this scenario because I have been there. I actually raised my "office manager's" pay well above what it should have been because of this. A true office manager should be the highest-paid non-producer in the office. Incorrectly titled employees are often making far more money than they should.

Is your office manager paid correctly? Is your total payroll expense below 25 percent of collections?

Another question I get with office managers often is "Should I let them do payroll? I am concerned because they aren't the highest-paid non-producer." The answer becomes obvious when you understand the dynamics—the employee has the wrong title. Yes, anyone doing payroll should be the highest-paid non-producer.

The second problem comes with resumes. The term *office manager* is so widely used incorrectly that when you search for one in dentistry, you can get anyone from a glorified receptionist to a manager who has run multiple offices at once. Separating the wheat from the chaff can be difficult until you know what to look for and what to ask.

## So How do you find the right manager?
## Ask the right questions.

I wonder if you can relate to this: my first office manager had actually never hired, disciplined, or fired an employee before. She had never managed payroll. She had twenty years of experience in an office that was collecting $350k. I had hired someone who was holding me back because she did not know anything different, and the experience she did have actually worked against growth. Running a $350k office is completely different than running a $700k office or a $1-2M office. She also accepted well under $20 per hour, which should have really clued me in on her skill set. Later, I also learned that she did not have the personality to be able to manage. She was just not the right person for the job, and I did not know it at the time.

So, first, you need to ask what specific tasks they did in their previous position. Do these it coincide with the tasks you want them to do, or were they an incorrectly titled employee?

Second, and likely the most important for any position in the office: what is their natural behavior leading them to do? No one is good at everything. Dentists, for example, are often Type A personalities, extremely detail-oriented, and due to a high level of education, often don't think outside the box as much. These qualities tend to make us great at dentistry, but often also make us micro-managers who hold our teams back from growth. Being a good team leader or manager typically requires someone who is more goal-oriented, does not micromanage, and can inspire team motivation. The Culture Index or Kolbe are good tools to find out what qualities your applicants have and can help you see if they will fit a specific job category or not. These are not tools to measure the candidate as a "good" or "bad" employee, but rather their specific role and potential fit in your practice's team.

Finally, you need to look at what kind of office the candidate worked in before. Large offices come with very different dynamics than smaller ones, which necessitate different skills. Insurance vs. FFS offices tend to look very different from each other as well. Now, if you have the right candidate with personality and attitude, then these differences are not going to be reasons to avoid hiring someone. However, they are good indicators of what type of training and experience they have had and what you will need to work on when training or retraining them to fit your office and needs.

What do you look for when hiring employees—especially an office manager? Finding a good office manager or any employee for your business is hugely important; they can either be one of your greatest assets or a total liability. That's why a robust interview and screening process is essential at the hiring stage. Does your office really need an office manager, or do you need another position, like a patient coordinator or treatment coordinator?

# Chapter 7
# Image and Presentation

I have always been told I look young for my age; people still occasionally ask if I am old enough to be a dentist. At the time of writing this book, I am thirty-five, have been married ten years, and have owned the office almost that long as well. Great problem to have, right? Well, on a personal level, this is a great thing to have, but on the business side, it can be a concern. My first couple of years in the office, I wore scrubs. Almost daily, I had patients ask either jokingly or seriously, "Are you old enough to be a dentist?" I could tell it really affected the perception patients had of me, and my treatment acceptance rates were lower because of it. It did not help my confidence level, either.

It is amazing how much success comes from those who present themselves well. I started wearing business attire two years in, and a magical thing happened. I was getting daily questions of "Are you old enough?" When I changed my appearance, those questions stopped almost completely. My treatment acceptance also increased noticeably, and office production increased significantly.

Now, I am not suggesting everyone wear business attire; it really depends on the look and feel you want in the office. It also has a lot to do with the appearance of the doctor. Like with me, a doctor with a young appearance would likely do better with more formal attire to help increase the age perception. On the other hand, a pediatric office might be better with scrubs to connect with kids. An office that wants to focus more on cosmetics or high-end care is likely to not do as well in scrubs. This is something that really needs to be evaluated when you start the office to make sure it all blends with the overall goals and vision of the business. Know who your patients are and the image that will resonate the most with them.

The same would go for your team as well. A dress-coordinated office presents itself a lot better than one where everyone is wearing something different. There are multiple ways to accomplish this. Some choose to have everyone in the same scrubs. You could also have the front team dress in matching business attire, or matching, monogrammed jackets. The point is more that you choose some coordination between team members, than what that coordination specifically looks like.

What kind of image do you want your staff to portray? What kind of image would your patients expect?

If you aren't sure where to start in this realm, hiring an image consultant can go a long way. These are experts in not only how to convey a message, but also in how to get teams to understand the need for it. There is something important to be said in the psychology behind what image you present and the message it sends. Many of us will spend a fortune in marketing and design, only to forget about the message that is sent in the office, which may be completely different than what is advertised.

Are these concepts ones your office might need to evaluate? Are you united and consistent in the image you are portraying to your patients? What expectation of you do they have before they are even sitting in your chair?

# Chapter 8
# Collections and Policies

Have you ever had the feeling that you were producing a ton, patients were coming in a lot and getting work done, but you just never seem to have turned the profits your work should have garnered?

Producing is often not a problem we have as dentists; we can have fun working on teeth all day long. Yes, most people tend to think we are a little crazy for that, but we enjoy it. However, we need to remember that we are also running a business, and getting paid for our work is just as important as doing the work in the first place.

I have yet to find an office I have coached that has not had an issue with collections when I first looked into their practice. Now, these issues could be large or small, anywhere from 95 percent to 60 percent. The problem and solutions all tend to be the same, just on different scales. There is a breakdown somewhere in the system and team between how the patient gets scheduled and treated to how the patient pays for that treatment.

### Delta Dental Phenomenon

I only mention Delta because they are traditionally the main insurer with the policy to send a claim check to the patient instead of the out-of-network provider. This makes them one of the largest concerns for dental offices that are out of network with them because they aren't handling the patient correctly on the front end.

Have you ever tried to get that money from a patient if they cashed the check the insurer sent them? It ranges anywhere from highly difficult to near impossible. The near-impossible cases are often because some patients have learned this and intelligently scam dental offices out of payment by knowingly getting treatment done and keeping the check. These are the worst offenders to keep track of, and having good collections policies in place will prevent them from making you their next scam. Even being in-network, I have suffered a few "errors" when Delta treated us like we were OON and sent the check to the patient. Over time, I had to develop a few things to stop this. I have changed our financial agreement consent form to be clearer and more supportive of collections law and agencies. My team has changed how we talk to patients about their insurance and payment. Finally, I have changed not only how patients pay but also what fees get tacked on that pay potential collections agents to incentivize the patient to prevent us from needing to get them involved in the first place.

What could you do to improve your business's collection rate? What's holding you back from making improvements?

## Fear of Upsetting Patients

I hear a lot that dentists are hesitant to either create or enforce a cancellation policy or prepayment policy. There is often a fear that creating any policy is going to upset their patients into leaving. Usually, setting up some kind of policy will pay off in many ways. Think of a few things. First, can you think of many businesses that set appointments that do not have a cancellation policy? Think of good hairdressers, or your physician, or your airline. Most businesses have policies that help guide clients to keep their commitments. It just makes business sense to protect your schedule and time. Second, I believe that most of us desire to be respected. If you don't respect yourself enough to try to put a value on your time, why do you think your patients will?

And lastly, the fear that you might lose patients by sticking to a policy. For this point, I want you to think about the nature of people in general. You will have 20 percent of people who make your life very easy; they are pleasant, stick to commitments, and are generally positive to be around. You have the opposite 20 percent that no one wants to be around—they are always negative, they find fault with everything, they don't like their lives, and they like blaming everyone else around them. And then you have the rest of the population that fits somewhere in between. Your patients are going to fit this same mold. The negative 20 percent are going to be the patients who make your life miserable. You know the day will be more difficult when you see them on the schedule. They make your collections team member stressed, are the ones that respect no one else's time, and are usually your schedule breakers. Do you really think these patients are going to be assets to the office that make you money? Of course not!

But wait, patients refer other patients; I don't want to break a potential referral source! Think about it. People hang out with people like themselves. Do you really want your negative, stressful patients to refer more people like them? Who in turn, will refer even more negative, stressful patients? It can be a vicious cycle but one that you can avoid if you have respectful but clear expectations set on the part of both the dentist and the patient. Not all patients are good to have in the office!

## Cancellation Policies

If you would like a starting point, here is our policy on patients and appointments. I have never once had to dismiss a patient for scheduling issues, since this policy tends to account for any type of patient. Feel free to use or modify it, but I can tell you this has worked extremely well for us.

1. Forty-eight hour notice

We used to do twenty-four, but so many patients called the day before, often at like fifteen minutes before we closed about an 8 a.m. appointment the next day and think that still meant twenty-four hours. Some people really have a hard time understanding basic math. Last I checked, sixteen hours is less than twenty-four hours. Therefore, we went to forty-eight hours because now you can be "nice" if you want, but you get at least one full business day to fill the slot, which is what you really want.

2. $50 per hour fee

We used to do $25 flat, but $25 is not enough to cover a hygienist's loss of time. I do per hour because not all appointments are an hour long. Amazingly, patients actually seem to respect a higher fee more. We might go to $75 in the future if we continue to have problems. However, I can tell you we got far more of the response we wanted from patients when we upped the fees. Making it a per-hour fee helps as well, mostly on the doctor's schedule or any longer procedure.

3. First offense = warning

I train my team to start with this on a patient's first missed appointment: "I understand life gets in the way. As a courtesy, I have permission to waive the first $50 short-notice cancellation fee for you today only, but I won't be able to do so again. What is a good day/time to get you back on the schedule so you can get 'XYZ' treatment done that is important due to 'ABC' reason? (set time) Great. If your plans change, will you please let me know with at least forty-eight hours' notice so we can help you avoid any cancellation fees?" (Wait for the verbal commitment.)

4. Second offense = charge

Use similar wording to the first about rescheduling. (If this is doctor time, you might want to move ahead to the next point. Hygiene time, you have your costs covered.)

5. VIP patient / Pre-op patient

Some patients just need to be reclassified. "It sounds like you have a busy life. I would love to help you avoid more fees. Would it be easier for you to call us the day you know you have some available time to come in instead of scheduling ahead?"

If Yes - "Great, I will put you on our VIP list for those with busy lifestyles. This should help you avoid any future cancellation fees. Please call us first thing in the morning when you have a day you are available, and we will do our best to get you on the schedule if we have time."

If NO – We will reschedule hygiene since the fee is high enough to cover costs, but all future doctor visits become pre-pay or pre-op first.

If you don't already have these policies and systems in place, give some thought to what would work best in your office. Then make sure you write it down and make it available to your staff and patients.

6. Pre-Op visits

These visits are for the patients who are just plain unreliable. A vast majority of the reasons given are either money or a lack of time management, and we need to help them see us as a priority. Ask for payment in full the day of diagnosis. If they pay in full, book them like normal. If they are resistant:

Okay, when would you like to schedule for your pre-op appointment? We will check and make sure everything is still good to go, go over consents, answer any questions you might think of, and take care of financing on that day. Would this week or next work better for you?

Pre-op appointments are set in the overflow column, so an assistant or front team member sees them. The doctor might pop in if the patient has a question, but otherwise, they're no reason to affect the dentist's schedule. During these visits, you take vitals, review treatment, go through consents, and then collect payment in full. Then schedule the actual treatment time. If they no-show a pre-op appointment, we lose nothing at all and can avoid charging a fee.

People will naturally follow their own money. If you have the patient's money, you will remove all but the most unavoidable reasons for a patient not showing up.

What about potentially upsetting a positive patient that you would otherwise want to keep? Well, for one, I will say in most circumstances that your good, positive, paying patients will not try to disrupt your schedule. I have dozens of stories about this, but here is one of the most enlightening ones that really changed my outlook on cancellation policies a few years ago.

I had a patient who wanted four veneers, for which she prepaid. She rescheduled her first three-hour veneer appointment due to a stomach bug. She had already rescheduled on the hygiene schedule before that, and we have a policy to only let the first one slide.

But it is a $5,000 case; don't want to upset them, right? We let the first veneer appointment cancellation slide without charging as a courtesy.

The patient had rescheduled for another day. She called again that morning to try to cancel, this time due to a migraine. This time we held our ground and said, "Sorry, but a three-hour appointment is a lot of time, and we are unable to treat other patients today because you reserved that time. In order to cancel that appointment, we would have to charge."

Well, her husband had come in for his hygiene visit in the morning and told us the patient was upset, and he did not seem happy, either. It was not fun but I had to tell him there was nothing I could do; this was the third time and we had already let her slide twice.

So, instead of paying a cancellation fee, the patient decided to come. My assistant asked how she was feeling. "Just fine." If I could roll my eyes in text, here would be the time. She was very anxious about the treatment, though, and did have a fair amount of questions. Otherwise, the visit went smoothly, and she was happy with the results.

Of course, now I know the "migraine" was just stress, and now I even wonder if the stomach bug was anxiety as well. Either way, getting prepayment AND sticking to a cancellation policy helped us stay on schedule and get the anxious patient past her issues. The policy ended up being a win for both the patient and us.

So stay strong, and develop and stick to a good policy! It is worth it and it does pay off. The only patients you will ever run off aren't patients you want to keep anyway.

This is one of those concepts I learned early but took forever to actually implement. I felt bad about judging patients and treating some different than others. I had to learn the hard way that not only was I the one holding us back with this concept, but also the patients actually do better, like you more, and follow through with more care when you do learn to NOT treat every person the same.

It all has to do with personalities—not every patient responds the same way to a stimulus. Just like treatment plans, not every patient will respond the same to office policy. It is important to treat every personality with the appropriate guidelines and not be afraid to stick to those guidelines for the well-being of everyone.

A great book to read on this is *The Five Love Languages*. It is a good illustration on a personal level of how people respond differently to each other.

# Chapter 9
# Maintaining the Schedule

O nce you set a solid collections and cancellation policy, you won't have to deal with most of the scheduling problems. You may end up with some of the less common ones.

One day I got a message from one of my receptionists:

"Patient called, has a hole in his mouth and needs an extraction and wants to know when would be a good time to come in. I looked in his treatment plan and I don't see anything about an extraction. I let the patient know that you would look at chart/X-rays to see if you see anything. The patient doesn't want to ask for time off work and not get any treatment. Please call the patient."

Do you ever have this scenario happen? At first I was fairly upset. What are we going to find in the chart that is not already there? And then I realized this was not necessarily a fault with the receptionist, but with her training. Train the receptionists to realize their number one goal is getting patients scheduled. If you roleplay scenarios like this with them during training, you can avoid a lot of potential dropped balls and headaches for your team and yourself.

The patient even said they don't want to take time off work twice, even better! They are likely to be willing to put a deposit on that appointment so you can lengthen it to give enough time to do the treatment. The deposit goes towards their treatment costs. In one hour, you can do almost anything on an emergency basis: extraction, filling, or pulp a tooth to start an RCT. If you aren't comfortable with that, make it ninety minutes and increase the deposit. Again, the overall point is that the receptionist needs to do whatever she can to get the patient scheduled.

Set the standard, train your team. Same-day treatment is a big key to increased production! Unless a patient specifically asks to talk to the doctor AND you have exhausted every possible option, just schedule the patient. The dentist should never be calling patients to make appointments. We should have better things to do, like treating the ones that we did get scheduled.

## Scheduling Lab Cases

Have you ever had your assistant come to you and say, "I have tried calling this patient several times to get their crown seated, and I cannot get them to answer"? How about your receptionist complaining that Mrs. Jones has called four times to check and see if her case is ready when you just prepped it last week? It happens far more often than it should in many offices.

Keeping track of lab cases and keeping patients coming in was an issue for me a few years ago. Eventually I decided I should make my life easier and not deal with having to contact them after the fact.

Patients want confidence and usually dislike the unknown. Waiting to schedule the patient only once the case arrives causes a lot of potential problems. So, why not just schedule crown seats the day you prep? Most labs will give you a calendar timeline that helps a ton with this effort. I started scheduling for two days after the expected delivery date. This gave my team time to check the schedule the day before the appointment and make sure the case had arrived.

This has some potential problems as well, but from my experience, these issues are easier to solve because they are internal problems. Assistants need to check the next day's appointments daily and make sure all cases are delivered. If not, first call the lab, and only call to reschedule the patient if the lab somehow cannot get it to you by the appointment time. The team needs to make sure to document every call in the chart journal. This allows all the other team members to be able to keep track or know what is going on should a patient call to ask.

After a few reiterations, we created a lab tracking sheet to make sure the assistants would not let a case fall through the cracks. This sheet became even more important if patients fell off the schedule or did not pre-book a seat appointment. We keep it posted inside the cabinet door where lab cases are stored. This way, assistants can immediately see an inventory of everything that is in, when it is scheduled, and when it has been delivered and crossed off the list. Many practice software programs have something similar, but my team specifically worked better with paper tracking where the cases were stored.

If a patient does not want to pre-schedule or somehow falls off the schedule, the team will call three times and then send an email. Typically, this takes care of most cases. The final check we instituted is a call/email from the doctor directly with a warning that the case may no longer fit and need to be redone if they do not come ASAP.

Finally, we organized cases by the day they are to be seated. We have boxes for each day on the schedule and then an overflow box (for unscheduled cases). Once a case is checked in, it is put in the box for the day of the week the patient is scheduled. On the day of seating, the assistant only has to check the one box to pull all the cases out for the day, instead of the large box of every case. This really saves time!

Labs have been a past major frustration for me, but since we made these changes, it has no longer been an issue.

Could you put a similar policy in place? Would that make a difference in your office? What other concerns with scheduling are you encountering that could use a solution?

# Chapter 10
# **Overspending**

E ight years in, most things were going great. Most of my systems had been in place and working well for quite some time. The office had grown consistently every year. My team was taking care of most of the day-to-day chores while I could focus more on business and growth. The office was collecting almost $2 million each year.

What could possibly go wrong? If you have been reading this story straight, you know there is a problem coming up. It was never one I noticed much, but over the years, it added up to be a huge burden. I wonder if you can relate to this.

My loan payments were eating up over two-thirds of my profit each month, all because of one of the most common and most insidious problems dentists tend to face—overspending. It is so easy to spend more money as a dentist because in most situations, the bank is eager to give us more money. Dental offices have one of the lowest failure rates of any industry. In many ways, however, I believe we are also hit with a higher-than-average marketing campaign for our profits. We tend to have a high cash flow, and yet most of us are not trained to deal well with finances. It was only after I saw the huge issues of multiple little problems racking up over the years that I truly appreciated how bad loans on non-essential things can be. Hopefully, you can see some of these issues before they happen to you.

## CAD/CAM and Large Equipment Purchases

Are you a believer in CAD/CAM? Contrary to what some may think, I am not against CAD/CAM at all. Digital impressions are a great idea; however, I do have a few words of caution you might want to think about before jumping into this highly expensive realm.

Three years in, I was convinced to give CAD/CAM a second chance. One of the reps I still work with today was rather surprised because I told him when I first met him that I was completely against the idea. Baylor had not given us a good experience with the systems, and most of the instructors were uncomfortable with the technology at the time. Therefore, I graduated with the opinion I would never do CAD/CAM.

I at least did one smart thing—I demoed two systems in the office on patients I had worked with for years. I got a very good feel for each system and found the one that worked better for us. I am a natural with computers and technology, so picking them up was simple. Most of the training went into getting my team accustomed to it and then learning to prep teeth differently to match what the system needed, which is different than standard prep design.

Of course, as I'm sure you're aware or will soon learn, the reps for the companies really know how to push their products and often spout a ton of baseless information. Even only three years out, I was fairly skeptical when some rep tried to oversell a product's usefulness. Below are some of the points I was told.

"CAD/CAM will let you sell more indirect restorations."

If you have a lot of in-network patients, be cautious of this tactic. Unless you really believe in inlays and onlays, or you have a silver tongue, it is a massive uphill battle to try to get an in-network patient to pay more out of pocket to save a minimal amount of tooth structure. Sadly, most patients just don't care about many of the things we do. Most of the time, all they want is dentistry done cheaper, faster, and less painful.

Personally, I was not on board with upselling a patient's out-of-pocket expense to get a restoration that insurance rarely covers. Expect most to downgrade to a filling for their portion, leaving you with a cheaper restoration or a patient needing to pay even more than just a standard crown. If you are FFS, by all means go for it here; conservative is good.

"CAD/CAM saves you money."

Yes, the true cost of a crown with a mill is less than $50, so this savings depends on the lab you currently use. You can get quality lab products in the range of $100–$150 per unit. So yes, you can save $50–$100 per crown, which can be a savings of $1,000–$3,000 per month. However, also realize all the other costs that will come with that. You are now tied to having to train assistants to use it. This is a problem if your assistant does not stay with you for several years or more, because training is expensive and only included at the beginning. You are going to be paying more for an assistant's paycheck and potential chair time. The design and milling take a lot more time because someone has to do it in the office. And finally, you have the cost of replacement burrs and maintenance on the equipment. When I finally looked at all of this a couple years later, CAD/CAM had actually saved me nothing. If you are considering investing in CAD/CAM, I highly recommend you scrutinize exactly how much it will cost your business.

"Marketing for CAD/CAM can get you more patients."

This is the one statement that has a lot of truth to it; however, be aware that means you really need to learn how to market both internally and externally for the technology to reap the benefits of the technology.

I gave the technology a try for three years, and overall I wish I had not wasted the money. I know some people who have made it successful, but most I have talked to have been lackluster or sold it.

In summary, be cautious. As with any other large equipment purchase, you really need to evaluate whether you *want* the technology. It is a complete mental shift to really make it successful. Do not buy into the idea that it will save you money unless you have a multiple-doctor office. All of the dentists I have talked to who have made it successful also reiterated that it never saved them money when they account for everything. And because it is not a money saver, I would not recommend most dentists get it until your other loans are paid off. My one big regret with CAD/CAM was not when I tried it out—it was in the loan and interest costs I had to pay later.

The takeaway message is this: Don't spend large amounts of money on equipment that you can practice dentistry without until you are debt free.

## Lab Bills

It is only fitting that I move to labs from CAD/CAM. Having been a past CAD/CAM user, I can tell you that I am a much happier provider not needing to deal with it. A lot of that is from lessons I learned through working with the technology and then needing to come back to the more traditional to solve some of the problems that caused me to look at CAD/CAM to begin with.

One of the main reasons I started with CAD/CAM was lab bills. Being a mostly in-network office, we were spending $200–$300 and sometimes more on crowns. The lab I was working with was great, but when you are only getting paid $600–$700 with some insurance companies, spending close to half of that on labs was not working out well. The pendulum swinging the opposite direction did not work either. I tried multiple labs that were under $100 and ended up spending far more on time, effort, and supplies, and also lost patients due to low-quality work. The sweet spot I have found is around $100–$150 per unit. I have found that multiple labs provide a quality product in that range, which was about half of what I was spending a few years prior. Cutting your lab bill in half has potential for you in the long run.

I still use the more expensive lab, but only on cosmetic cases and only when the patient is willing to pay for the difference. Personally, I like using local labs because I want custom staining for anterior work and next-day delivery of dentures used as custom trays.

Overall, it is important to find someplace that can deliver a consistent, quality product for a moderate price.

## Supplies

Be willing to evaluate your investment versus returns on the supplies that you need. This does not come at the expense of your patient, but instead ensures that the needs of both you and the patients are being met. Evaluate the products available and make informed decisions with regard to the cost/benefit analyses.

This is one of my love-hate relationships in dentistry. There are some products I know I will never switch away from. A good example is my crown cement, which has been one of the most consistent products I have ever used. If I spend a little more on it vs. an off-brand cement, great. It saves me a ton of time and hassle. As with probably most of you reading this, my composite is the same. You will likely pry it from my arthritic hands only after I retire.

That being said, there are many things you can use off-brand and still get the same results. Here is the hate part of the relationship with supplies tracking. Do not let the cost of finding the savings overshadow the savings themselves.

Quality—As I mentioned with cements and composites, there are just some things that are not worth sacrificing quality. For each of us, that might be different, but don't let trying to save money actually cost you more because you have to replace your work.

Time—I have worked with offices that actually spent several hours a month trying to save money on supplies. They would order from multiple companies and search through several catalogs, all in order to save minor amounts of money. There is a point at which the savings you get do not outweigh the cost to get them. Remember, you or a team member spends each of those hours. Your team costs money per hour, and that time might be much better spent elsewhere. Inventory control should not take more than a couple hours a month to handle at most. A good rule is that for every hour your team spends trying to save money, they should at minimum save you five times their salary. This is because you can likely get that much or more out of them doing something else in the office.

Budget—Your supply budget should be 3–4 percent of your monthly collections. Remember this, because saving 10 percent on supplies only saves 0.4 percent of collections. If you otherwise spent that time and energy in increasing production, which would pay off more? In most cases, spending one hour a week productively can increase your production by 10 percent. I don't know about you, but I would rather have 10 percent than 0.4 percent. Even with an overhead of 60 percent, that is still a tenfold increase in gain, which is substantial! Remember the discussion about fixed expenses from Chapter 3? An increase in production after fixed expenses are paid is much more profitable.

Overall, yes, saving money is a good and important thing to do as a business, but do remember that you also need good value for your efforts. This typically means that value per time spent usually puts supplies as one of the lower items on your radar to try to reduce costs. This does not mean you don't try; it just means you should spend more energy and time on almost every other expense control measure.

A great place to start is with a group of dentists who have already found the solutions. Nifty Thrifty is a great online community where dentists share their best savings tips that don't require a lot of time to find or implement.

## Equipment

There are so many expensive toys in dentistry that we can spend money on. For many dentists, a lot of them end up in the closet collecting dust after a few years, just like that exercise bike that becomes an expensive clothes rack, or the sandwich-toasting machine that makes one toasted sandwich and then never gets used again.

The main goal is to make sure that when you spend money on equipment, it will not end up being that dust collector. Here are a few questions you should probably ask yourself before you buy any new piece of equipment.

What is the cost-benefit? Will it save or make me money quickly? Most of the work we do in dentistry has not changed in decades. Crowns and fillings are still the same. Materials might have changed slightly, but the overall process is the same as it was last generation. Yes, you can do things with digital, but how much will that improve the process for you? And if it does improve the process, will that improvement give you a return fast enough to justify the cost?

What is the opportunity cost? If you are taking out a loan, be sure to factor the cost of interest payments into the cost of the new purchase. If you have a limited budget, you may also want to consider if you buy your new purchase, is there anything that you would be prevented from buying instead? A good example is marketing. If you have to cut into your marketing budget to buy something, you might want to make sure the new equipment is going to get you at minimum a 3:1 fast return on the investment, or you may have a lost opportunity cost.

Am I willing to go all-in with it? Is this something I really believe in using?

If you need to be convinced something is a good thing, it probably isn't. When you are not gung-ho about a new product, it might not be the right product for you. Also remember your team as well, since most new equipment also requires their training and correct use as well. Don't be afraid to say no to something new and shiny if those are its only positives.

A good, personal example of this is solar panels. A couple years ago, I had a friend start a solar panel business, so he was giving them out at half price to get a few good recommendation clients. When we looked at the cost even at half price, it would have taken eight years just to earn back the cost of the panels. If we paid for it in cash, there was a compounding 8 percent lost opportunity cost because that was our average return on personal investments at the time. If we paid through a loan, that would have been an increase of 5 percent, which compounds over time and made that eight years even longer. Sure, I like the idea of solar energy, but I did not care enough about it to spend so much money to try it. And finally, my wife did not like the appearance of the panels, and none of the other virtues made sense when I might have to hear her complain for years about the appearance of our roof.

New equipment can be a great thing if it satisfies all the questions, or it might turn into one of the worst things you ever wasted money on if you ignore the red flags.

For those who are opening a new office or moving, I recommend also reading the chapter on office design because it also goes into a lot of detail about purchases and organization.

I have worked in two offices now, and if I had designed the first office any way like my second, I would have saved all the moving and contracting costs of needing to fix the problems. Doing it right the first time would have saved me several hundred thousand dollars. How would you like to have an extra few hundred thousand dollars? Would that make a huge difference in your life?

## Contracts

Here's another hard lesson learned. I worked with a merchant service company a few years ago. They had a two-year contract with auto-renewal every year after. The main issue with the renewal, however, was that they only allowed you to cancel within one month of the renewal date. Otherwise, if you were unhappy with them during eleven months out of the year, you were screwed. After three years, well past their initial period, I decided I needed a change for various reasons, and ended up needing to hire a lawyer to get me out of the contract. It was a huge nightmare to deal with, all because the company does not understand there is no reason to keep an unhappy client other than creating negative reviews.

The only contracts I will ever sign nowadays have a maximum of one year, no auto-renewal. I urge you to do the same. Month-to-month is good because you can get out at any time. If someone cannot prove their value in a year, that tells me everything I need to know about them before I waste my time and money. I have found that this policy helps a lot with guiding me towards not wasting my efforts looking into questionable companies. I have always found alternative options with companies that understand happy customers renew happily and therefore don't need long-term contracts.

## Conclusion

If I had learned some of these lessons a few years ago and not overspent a ton, I would be much better off. I would have been debt free in half the time, which means I would be taking home three times as much in half the time. It is good to be vigilant about whether you need that new piece of equipment, or whether you should spend money on that new project. Always keep in mind how important it is to spend that money wisely, and if you are still going to like having that purchase five or ten years later. A great resource for any dentist is to have a sounding board, someone who has been there before and can help you brainstorm about whether your next purchase is going to be a success or a waste.

Be open to feedback and be sure to adequately examine the real costs that any new purchases or technology may have outside of the initial financial investment.

# Chapter 11
# **Stress**

S tress can be a killer. And anything you can do to reduce your stress has got to be a good thing.

I had my deepest pit of stress in running the office about six years in. My loans and overspending had really racked up and were taking almost 70 percent of my profit. I found out the IRS still taxes the entire amount, so even though I was running an office collecting well over a million dollars, at the end of the day, I was taking home only about 10 percent of it. I was working five days a week. I rarely went home without having one or two hours of work still to do, from notes to dealing with other business decisions. I was not getting time to enjoy being at home or with family. I rarely took a vacation because I felt like I could not afford to take off and leave the office. My long-term assistant moved out of state, making my CAD/CAM unit nearly useless or highly time-consuming. Team issues were constantly on my mind. With all this going on, most people can probably understand why I opened a Heartland Dental corporate office letter and picked up the phone, looking into details of selling the office.

Well, obviously, I did not sell. But how close I came is one of the reasons I love helping other dentists avoid getting to this tipping point. Large amounts of stress are not a requirement for our career. I would say stress actually makes us less good at our job, so here are several ways to get to a point that will give you minimal stress.

## Time Management

So how many of us can say we work four days a week or less, never bring work home with us, and are very successful?

I don't know about you, but when I heard that years ago, I thought something was fishy or they were exaggerating. After several years of being in that scenario, I can tell you it actually is very possible. All without gimmicks, over-diagnosing, or breaking your back. And it can be done just as well with PPO or FFS.

First steps: Think about how much time you spend in the office doing nothing or doing something that is not highly productive. What if you took that same amount of time and were producing dentistry at a pace you like? How often are you doing something that can be done by another team member? There are so many things ONLY we can do, so we need to focus on those tasks. Learning to train and delegate the rest is the ticket to less stress and more productivity.

Having consistent great months and being efficient and productive are the best ways to hold back the advance of corporate dentistry or any other competition we have. They cannot compete with private practice on service and compassion. The main reason corporate offices survive in dentistry is their systems. There is no reason a private practice cannot have similar systems and also have the personal care and service corporate cannot provide.

So, what are some things you have done to make your office run efficiently and smoothly? What are some areas of concern for you that. if they were fixed, would make a big difference in your professional life? A lot of this was trial and error for me. Once I finally saw some of the little things I delegated worked better without my constant input, it made me want to delegate more and more. Over time, I noticed I am much happier not dealing with the minutia because I have seen it work without me and I have time to spend on bigger and better projects.

What would you like to NOT have to do anymore that is legally possible to delegate?

It all starts with recognizing the things holding you back and finding ways to improve on them.

The biggest stress point I had was employment concerns. Once I finally got my team managing themselves and gave my office manager the training and authority to take care of the rest, my stress from team issues almost completely disappeared. Now, I usually hear of problems after they have already been solved. I go into a lot more detail about how to get there in the chapter on team development. Setting up systems in this realm and being able to back off reduced my largest source of stress and helped make running the office a much easier task.

Patient concerns can be another stress point, especially when they write a public negative review. But almost as bad are the ones who leave and don't post a review, but you know they are telling everyone they know instead. Learning not only how to respond to patient concerns and reviews, but also learning how to avoid them having the problems in the first place reduced another huge point of stress for me.

Finally, learning to be more financially successful and profitable helps a ton. It is amazing how much more fun work can be when you are paid a lot more to do it. Avoiding all the overspending, paying off your loans, and learning to be more efficient can help you get paid far more for the same amount of work. Sounds good, right?

The next chapter will start with the most stress-relieving point for me: team development.

# Chapter 12
# Team Development

I know most of us would say that the most stressful thing about running an office is managing employees, especially when it comes to having to discipline or fire one. You are not alone. I have yet to meet anyone who enjoys disciplining or firing people who work for them, we develop an emotional attachment to the people we work with. However, there are multiple ways to help make this a better experience for both you and your employees.

## Always Know the Laws

One of the main sources of discomfort for dentists is being unsure of the laws that you have to follow so that you can be confident in the choices you want to make. Every state is a little different, however many states follow similar trends or rely on federal regulations. It is good to have an attorney to answer questions; but most situations are simple, and some HR courses and education can help you avoid the much larger cost of constantly needing your attorney.

- There are several classes of employees protected by law including sex, religion, gender, culture, sexual orientation, and age. These are never the reason to let someone go.

- Most states are "at will" employment, meaning the employer or employee may terminate the relationship at any time without reason.

- You do not have to have step-wise discipline or documentation to terminate an employee. There is nothing legally requiring them. If you have a toxic employee, get rid of them fast! Toxic employees will cost you far more in lost opportunity than anything else that might happen if you let them go.

- If you want to avoid unemployment, it is highly recommended to document and retain verbal and written warnings. Documentation should state that the employer tried to give the employee additional training and/or coaching; basically, that the employer did everything to retain the employee and show as many examples as possible that the employee's skills or behavior were the only issue. Do not call this counseling; there has been a lawsuit where the employer was sued for not having a license to counsel.

## Essential vs Non-Essential Job Functions

What can an employee reasonably ask the employer to change or modify for the job? This is always a misunderstood area that many employers, without knowing the exact rules, tend to fear. You cannot fire someone because of the protected classes, which often leads to employers keeping around for example a toxic pregnant employee because they don't know how to appropriately release them.

An important distinction that is helpful to understand is the need to define tasks that are essential and non-essential to a job position. You are required to make special accommodations for employees IF they are reasonable and considered **non-essential** parts of their job. You will always be able to require an employee to complete an **essential** part of their job regardless of the circumstances. Here are some of the most common issues to know so you can avoid problems or getting into an uncomfortable situation with an employee.

- Non-essential changes: A common example is where you have a pregnant employee who needs to use the bathroom multiple more times per day; you should allow her to take more breaks to do so. This would not affect her ability to perform her essential duties.

- Essential duties: If an employee is unable to complete their essential job duties, you are not required to keep them! But this does not mean you have to fire them either.

A common example concerns X-rays and pregnancy. Taking X-rays would be considered an essential part of their job description. You do not have to retain an assistant or hygienist if they don't want to take X-rays. However, here is a way you can work through this situation to the good of the employee and your practice. If an employee has concerns about X-rays, you should absolutely sit down and listen to their concerns. Once they are done discussing their concerns, you can bring up the fact that evidence does not support that providers get any exposure to X-rays when the equipment is used correctly.

Since taking X-rays is an essential part of their job, no one in their position could be working without taking X-rays. However, you can understand that they have a concern, and you would be willing to buy them a radiation monitor badge to wear if they would like for peace of mind. These badges are an employer's protection as well as helps employees with legitimate concerns to get over their fears. There are also lead aprons employees can wear to protect themselves if they need added peace of mind. This example would work the same way for an employee with concerns about nitrous. A system that is functioning and used properly will not expose the operator to nitrous oxide. And there are nitrous oxide monitor badges to wear as well.

- Medical Leave of Absence (MLoA). If the employee is still uncomfortable completing essential parts of their job after all the evidence and monitoring, their last option is to take an UNPAID medical leave of absence. To be clear, to keep coming to work they must complete their essential tasks, including all X-rays/nitrous as they usually would. If the employer has less than fifteen employees (as most dental offices), you are NOT required to save their job when they return. This allows you to give them a legal way to take off the time they want without having to fire them or paying unemployment.

- It is advisable to have the employee sign a request for a MLoA that states the start date.

- The one major rule you have to follow, though, is preventing discrimination. To do this, you need to make sure you treat all employees the same regardless of disability or condition. I have a clinical employee who had shoulder surgery and her doctor put her on full time off work for two months, and then half-time work for two months. We told her we could not let her work during that second phase at half time; there is no way we could find a constant replacement to work four hours a day. So she took a four-month unpaid medical leave of absence. She is an amazing employee, so we did keep her job available for her and she has been working with me ever since. The overall point, though, is that we would treat any employee the same regardless of disability.

I have had several pregnant employees over the years. The easy cases have been where the employee had been pregnant before in a dental office and realized there was no cause for concern. The more difficult and emotional cases are when an employee is hyper-vigilant about possible risks.

One of my assistants fit the latter category. She was finding lots of non-evidence-based fears online about being pregnant in a dental office. X-rays did not pose much of a concern when we bought her a radiation badge and a lead apron for the midsection. Nitrous was the main fear factor for this assistant. I have two assistants so often we could just rearrange them for nitrous cases; but that was not always possible, which made this issue about an essential job task. This scenario ended up causing a lot of anxiety for my assistant and honestly some frustration for me. Should I have been frustrated? Probably not. I understood where she was coming from and realize she did not have the level of education and knowledge I do. Fear of the unknown is one of the most common causes of anxiety.

We purchased a nitrous badge for both assistants and sent them in for testing after. I had the assistants set up a call with the safety company and after the explanation of the results, all the fears about nitrous have dissipated. The cost of a few test badges and an extra apron avoided months of organizational dilemmas with trying to rearrange schedules and duties. The team is happy and better understands the safety protocols we have in the office.

Overall, you want to assure your team that your main objective as an employer is to provide a safe working environment. However, you also understand the evidence and therefore can be confident when you give your employees data that support their safety and can alleviate their concerns. Your team wants a leader who cares about them and looks out for them as well. Listen to their concerns, acknowledge them, and then find data or alternatives that can alleviate the concern without being detrimental to the office or other team members.

Have you had a toxic employee you have kept too long? Has any employee tried to hold you hostage on a part of employment law of which you aren't fully knowledgeable? What would it mean to your team and stress to be able to have confident answers to these concerns?

## Coaching vs Discipline

I don't know many of us who enjoy disciplining or firing employees. It is not enjoyable for anyone involved on either side; however, it is a vital part of being a boss and a leader.

The ideal goal of course is avoiding the need to terminate anyone. One of the main things to remember is discipline should not be about punishment for doing something wrong. It should be about coaching and training employees to know how to do their job better. The attitude with which you go into an employee evaluation means everything. Go into the meeting pissed off at someone and it shows, everyone gets emotional, it gets out of hand, and no one is happy. Go into the meeting with a positive outlook that you are just trying to work out how to get everyone working better together and it will go smoother.

The sandwich technique is a common motivation tactic. You always want to start and end a conversation on a positive note. If you must discipline or correct someone's work or behavior, start off first with something they are doing well.

Next, talk about the issue involved. Avoid directing what the employee is not doing, but instead how it is affecting the atmosphere/job. Then ask how YOU can HELP them to resolve the situation. This will completely change the context of the conversation for the better. Avoid blaming or YOU statements because they just create defensiveness. If you want good results remember this is about coaching them to do better, not about discipline.

Lastly, you should always end on a positive.

Here is an example of an assistant who is having issues keeping track of lab cases:

> Suzie, you are great with patients and working with me chairside. We are getting some patient complaints though that their lab cases are taking too long to get seated. I noticed that we are not getting things out the day they are done or having them sit for days before the patient is called. What can I do to help you make sure to get these cases out the same day or next day, and then make sure we follow up with the patient when the case comes in?

(discuss)

> Okay great, I think we have a good place to start in having these systems in place so that our patients are taken care of to the best of our ability. Is there anything else you want to talk about while we are together?

Then document the conversation!

Notice that we avoided blaming Suzie. We avoided saying anything that might cause her to get defensive. And we used the term WE instead of YOU. The only employees who are going to have problems when you use a positive method are the truly toxic employees. But this can be a good thing as well because what is happening is the employee is basically telling you straight out, "I need to be allowed to find another job."

Do you discipline or coach your team members? Are you open to having the difficult conversations in a positive manner? How could you apply this method to your business? Have there been times in the past when using a method like this might have eased a situation?

## Termination

It will happen to all of us, multiple times. If we run a business, we will need to terminate employees. This can be a stressful or emotional time. It does help to realize you need to cut unproductive/ineffective employees in order to PROTECT the rest of your team and patients. Think about it, who is more important to you—your good patients and team members, or the toxic employee? Protect and serve the good by trimming the bad.

So let's talk about a few ways to make this a smoother process:

- Stay short, concise, and limit details. In most cases, the employee already knows it is coming. The less you talk the less chance someone gets emotional or causes a scene. When in doubt, a good answer to why is "things are just not working out".

- Document each conversation. Like clinical dentistry, employment rules are all about documentation.

- Have a witness, which can help avoid "he said, she said" arguments later.

- In your documentation, to avoid paying unemployment, you need both a log of problems and of training/coaching that was done to try to solve the issue. The stated reason for termination in the file should be something like insubordination or behaviors that are illegal or harmful to patient care. Something like "employee refuses to follow standard procedure after multiple training attempts, leading to patient safety issues," will often get the state to side with you if you have supporting documentation.

## Resignation

Any time you can get an employee to resign instead of being fired, life is much easier. The absolute most important part about a resignation though is getting it in writing with a date and having the employee sign it! This will release you from most legal and unemployment claims.

If you ever offer severance pay (one–two weeks of pay when someone leaves) it helps to have your office manual state that only employees who resign in good standing will receive it. Doing it this way will incentivize your employees to resign instead of making you fire them. You should never give extra money to someone that you are having to fire unless you are doing it for purely emotional reasons (you feel bad for them). And of course, most people will tell you that running a business with emotions is a bad idea. If YOU did your job right as a leader and gave the employee plenty of opportunities to get training and improve, then THEY did it to themselves and you cannot help them with their poor life choices. You can lead a horse to water, but you cannot force it to drink.

## Source of toxicity

We all can point to patients we see who come in with the concern, "I just don't understand why I keep having dental problems." But they do minimal home care, consume acid and sugar like they are water, and infrequently see a dentist. Do you have patients like that? Most of us do. They are often the main cause of their own problems, but they don't want to admit it or change anything to prevent it.

Another example we see in life is someone who asks why they cannot find a good spouse but have been divorced four times.

In both scenarios, at some point, the problem might be internal, not external. How many relationships have to end before someone realizes the problem is not the other person? How many dentists have to tell someone they need to floss before it sinks in?

The same goes for running an office. Unfortunately, often the person not seeing the big picture is the leader. If you are having a run of toxic or ineffective employees, it might be time to look at yourself and your office practices instead of blaming all the people who keep not working out. Here are a few things to think about:

- Are you recruiting the right people?
- Have you run a behavior test on new hires, and do you know what behavior profile you need for that job?
- Are you looking for attitude first and skills second?
- Are your interview skills up to par to ask the right questions and see red flags?
- Are you hiring people out of a desire to find the right person, or out of desperation because you NEED someone NOW? Are you "settling" for someone?
- Are there good systems in place that help someone be successful at the job, or are you just winging it?
- Do you have clear written expectations and job descriptions?
- Do you have a solid training protocol for helping new people? Written with pictures or video? (No, verbal is NOT adequate in most cases).
- Are you giving GOOD feedback on performance?
- Are YOU an easy or hard person to work for? Are YOU a consistent leader that always wants the same things that are predictable?
- Are YOU doing everything possible to help your team succeed?

- Are YOU emotionally stable at work?

These can be difficult questions to ask, but they are highly important to help you, as well as your team, function effectively and without drama. I have had to deal with most of these concerns myself; and some of them are far harder to admit than others.

In a previous chapter we talked about the marketing cycle and how it is actually affected by so much more than what ad we run. Much of that success can come from our team and how they are working.

Again, these are not simple answers of "look here" or "do this one thing." Team building is a multi-faceted topic that needs diagnosis as much as our patients do. In order to diagnose the problem, we often need to know what ideal or normal looks like. When evaluating your processes for team development you want to make sure you address these techniques:

1. Have a great team member acquisition ad and recruiting process.

2. Screen candidates by phone first.

3. Learn how to evaluate a resume for red flags.

4. Learn how to have an effective interview process and what questions to ask.

5. Portray an office that someone WANTS to work for over other offices nearby both in the ad and during the interview. Remember, the employee is interviewing you as well.

6. Test an employee's skills and knowledge before putting them on the clock. Most ways employers try to avoid unemployment with working interviews have no legal basis.

7. Get the entire team get involved so they can help find the red flags.

8. Develop a comprehensive training protocol, ideally with pictures and video.

9. Have CLEAR written goals and expectations for each position.

10. Develop a strong onboarding process for new team members and help them with integration into the team.

11. Learn to effectively communicate what you need from the team.

12. Find and remove toxic employees that may be running off your new people.

13. And most important, learn to be and effective team LEADER.

All of these are far more important than which ad to place where for a new team member. It does not matter where you look for people if you don't know how to handle them when you find the right ones. I have had employees come from other offices who are currently rock stars, but their previous environment did not allow them to succeed. I have also seen one toxic employee ruin an entire team of great people.

Rock stars looking for a job are rare because they often are so valued, they tend to stay at offices for years. And even when they are available, they are smart enough to look for multiple offers, so unless you can present the best working environment you will lose them.

More often you will find the "diamonds in the rough"; employees who have great untapped potential. These are employees who have a great personality but may have not become rock stars yet due to a lack of training or poor working conditions. The best part about these potential diamonds—if you give them a great environment in which you train and treat them well, they will have a lot of loyalty to you. Some of these people may not even be looking for a job in dentistry until you find them.

This often then brings up the issue of why employees leave jobs. Contrary to popular belief, the most important thing to most employees is not money. A survey has been done every year for decades and money is never the top three most important qualities in an employee staying at a job. The top reasons typically are: being appreciated; having clear goals/expectations; feeling they are valued and serve an important function; and friendly coworkers.

So next time you are looking for a new or replacement employee, you might want to first check if your office is capable of attracting and keeping the best quality people. And then make sure you know how to train them and keep them happy when you do. Otherwise, you may end up with a revolving door or "settling" for mediocre.

And the best part about being able to get quality people...you have the ability to release those who aren't up to standard.

## Develop a culture of self-management and critical thinking:

Managing employees can sometimes be like herding children. They don't see the big picture and they often have a hard time seeing beyond themselves. However, a lot of this has to do with the culture and training within an office. Your role as leader will become much easier if you can develop within your team members the ability to critically think for themselves.

As an example, a few years ago my car breaks down on the way to the office. I call my front team leader to let them know because AAA is ninety minutes away. The fire department nicely shows up and was able to make a temporary fix to the problem. My team lead shows up with two assistants. She and an assistant stay with my car, the other drives me to the office because I have a patient waiting for me.

Later, when I get time to think, I ask my team leader to make a basket for the fire department to thank them for their help. She tells me not only did she already think about it, they already took care of it before coming back to the office.

However, I still made a mistake in this scenario. I had to work through lunch that day on an emergency patient they added on. So at the end of the day, I told my team I was going to the shop to get a more permanent fix. My team leader asked me "Why did you not tell us that; we would have taken care of that for you during lunch."

Does your staff have the authority to help in that way? Are they empowered to go above and beyond?

My example is a little extreme, but situations like this happen every day in the office with patients who need a little extra care or assistance. Most of the time, I suggest something, they are already doing it or it is done. Why? Because I learned to avoid micromanaging them and instead get them to think for themselves for the desired result instead of the process. So when you train your team, do you focus more on results or procedure? You might be happy to see how often your team will surprise you if you give them freedom to mold the process to get a better result. It is common as a *dentist* to want to look into every minute detail; however, as an *employer*, this can be what causes us to be one of the major stumbling blocks of team growth.

Is your team self-managed or micromanaged? Are there any scenarios in your office where you may be holding the team back from their best performance? When has your team surprised you by going above and beyond without being told to? Did you verbally recognize their initiative and success?

# Chapter 13
# Office Design

How is your office designed? Has it been cobbled together, or is it designed for success?

When I signed my first lease, it was a seven-year lease. My original landlord was friendly and available for questions, and I always felt like it was a mutually beneficial relationship. Well, five years into the office, he sold to a new buyer. The new landlord had less personality than a rock, was not available for questions, and my rent was getting raised four times more each year than prior years for several reasons. Suffice it to say, I no longer had a good reason to stay put or renew a lease. If I had a well-designed office across the board, I probably would have stayed just to avoid all the stress and cost of moving, but over the years, I found all the problems that added up. The office was also outgrowing the five-op space, so I decided to move and build a new office.

If you ever look at designing or redesigning an office, I highly recommend you do not use a dental supplier. They are not trained in efficient design, and many of the things they try to design by default are there to help you spend more money with them in both equipment and supplies. My first office was designed by the supplier based on a standard design.

Having worked in both a standard office and an efficiently designed office, I would never go back.

A couple of years before I had to move, I went to a Breakaway seminar. Of all the seminars I have been to over the years, this one was one of the most useful. I highly suggest this seminar to any dentist owner. There were great management suggestions, but the most significant takeaway was the office design portion. Dental Ergonomics is the originator of many of the ideas; Breakaway expanded on them. While they are all great ideas, Breakaway focuses on associate-driven offices, meaning offices I don't think most of us would love working in as an owner. So here are a few concepts I recommend and have used in my office for both efficiency and pride in being an owner.

## Operatory Design

One of the most important changes is focusing on having an efficient operatory, since a majority of your space tends to be here. A standard operatory is 10 feet by 11 feet with side and rear cabinetry. However, I can tell you those side cabinets are completely useless. By now, I have seen hundreds of designs, and I have never seen a good reason to keep them except potentially in a single surgical suite. Everything that those cabinets are used for can be better done another way.

So why does this matter? Side cabinets take up a ton of space, all of which you pay for in both construction costs (by square foot) and rent. When you remove the side cabinets, you can remove up to twenty-two square feet per room, be more efficient, and have rooms that actually look and feel larger.

Is maximizing space important to you? One of the ways you still keep efficiency is in-wall cubby space. Each wall in a building has a ton of dead space within it. By putting a cubby built into the wall, you can gain this space back without sacrificing anything. You can mount anything you need in there: gloves, cleaning supplies, and even pop-up surfaces.

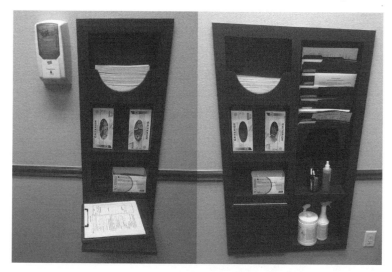

Computers today are much smaller and lighter than they used to be. My old office had full-size desktop computers that required a lot of cabinet space, were difficult to access, and needed good airflow to avoid overheating. In our new office, our computers are mounted below the upper cabinet. They have no issues with airflow, are much easier to access for USB port devices like X-ray sensors and intra-oral cameras, and do not require any use of cabinet space.

## Central vs. Operatory Storage

My first office was designed to store our supplies in each

room. The idea was that they are easily accessible when needed. The main problem that comes with this is inventory control. It is really depressing how many thousands of dollars of supplies I have thrown away over the years due to expiration or loss of equipment and supplies. When you store items in multiple places, you make inventory control exponentially harder for you or your assistant.

Central storage is a much more efficient way to handle supplies. The only supplies we store in a room either do not expire or are put in a clear organizer that is easy to see.

Every possible item is stored centrally and moved into the operatory as needed. The disposable organizers, instrument cassettes, and carts all get restocked centrally and then moved to rooms as needed. This allows fast setup of any room with easier restocking and inventory tracking, as well as allowing you to maintain less equipment and keep fewer supplies in stock. All of this can save you a ton of money over time. I recommend the use of anything you can do to keep inventory visible without spending time opening cabinets. This would include open shelving the and clear tip-out bins shown below. Simplastics is the only company I know that makes these for our purposes. They have a standard setup for dentists that is very easy to order.

On shelving, if you pre-mark the shelves to the max amount to store, anyone can easily see when you are getting under half inventory. Direct and visible indicators can simplify this process for your assistant or any other team member who needs to help determine when it is time to reorder.

## Reception Desk

How and when are your patients greeted? One general idea with almost any business is greeting clients as they enter the office.

When designing a check-in desk, it works best to make sure the receptionist can see someone when they enter and greet them immediately. However, when the patient sits down to wait, their focus should be taken away from the greeter so she can focus on the rest of her job. This is accomplished by both where the TVs and chairs are arranged, as well as where the greeter's desk is placed.

Overall, the new office design has not only saved a ton of construction money, but also allowed a more efficient use of space and a better flow. I highly suggest that anyone who is building or remodeling an office really think about taking some non-standard approaches that will pay themselves back over and over.

How you can capitalize on the space you have available? How you can make your environment work for you?

# Chapter 14
# Treatment Acceptance

After seven years of running the office, we had hit a small plateau. Collections increases each year were going up by less than 10 percent a year. Treatment acceptance was high, but not as good as it could have been. I started focusing this year on how to increase treatment acceptance. I focused on learning how to talk to patients even better, how to connect with them better, and ultimately how to get treatment acceptance higher.

It did not take long for my team to come to me and ask what was different, because the acceptance rate was significantly higher, and they were even noting fewer issues with collections and complaints. This year we increased by another 20 percent at the same time as lowering expenses and increasing profit significantly.

There are always new ways to improve your business. What could you do in your practice to increase treatment acceptance by 20 percent? What measures could you take today to reach that goal?

## Why Doctors Lose Patients: Not Listening

I had a great example patient come in last thing one day. This sweet eighty-year-old man had been seeing his dentist, whom he seemed to like, for ten years. He'd recently been told he needed a tooth removed (which he forgot until I talked about it) and had broken an acrylic partial of twenty years for the second time. His dentist told him it would be approximately $1,500 to replace it with a metal-based one so it would not break again. He came to me because he saw a mini-implant mailer and was looking for another option.

After talking to him, he liked his partial; it fit and functioned well for him until it broke. He had no need or budget for mini implants. The $1,500 was the main reason he did not get treatment with his current dentist, who he is likely to go back to for routine care. Since I listened to his concerns, we came up with the option of a simple extraction and a replacement acrylic partial for approximately $1,000. He came back the next day for thirty minutes, a $150 lab bill, and basically a $2,000/hour production all because I listened to his concerns and came up with a plan that fit his budget and lifestyle instead of just throwing him the "ideal" option.

I rarely talk to people about money specifics, but occasionally it does help when the patient's main concern is budget, because who is the best one to address concerns and possibly give alternate options? The dentist!

If you aren't getting 85 percent or more of your patients to get some immediate treatment acceptance, you might want to look at how and what you are presenting to patients. Partial plan acceptance is just fine; zero plan acceptances usually mean you missed the mark somewhere. The longer I do this, the more I realize that there is no "ideal" for every mouth. Each mouth is attached to a person. There is, however, an ideal for each patient. The problem comes in that there is no way for us to know what that ideal is until we talk to the patient and discover their life story and how dentistry relates to it. Too often, I notice I have tried to fit their life into the dentistry.

## Communication

I was in church one morning and could not stop thinking about how the sermon applied to dentistry. He talked about how marriage counselors say that most cases of dysfunction eventually boil down to one common theme: lack of communication.

Communication is both listening and speaking from both parties.

Thinking about our offices, we see many of the people we work with more than our spouses. They are all relationships, and no different than marriage in that they are only healthy with good communication.

Partnerships are business marriages and thrive or fail based on communication from both sides.

You have to communicate well with your employees to get them to do what you want. And almost all the failures in employment are because either you did not communicate/train well enough or they did not communicate/listen well enough.

Patient communication is usually the number one factor in treatment acceptance, treatment success, and happy patients.

When was the last time you focused on training/learning to be a better communicator? Learn to master this skill, and it will likely take you farther than any other skill you ever learn in your life and your career.

What situations can you think of in relation to your career or life where good communication helped, or better communication would have helped?

This depends on the patient. We always get X-rays and photos before I start talking about problems or treatment, so I have the general state of their teeth and their chief complaint already, and can start forming what I will be asking. Most people understand things far more easily when they can see it instead of just being told about it. Then, I let them talk about what they see, guiding them to see what I do.

The main idea is to TALK and TELL less than you ASK and LISTEN.

For instance, let's talk about an infected tooth.

"Hi, I see you have a painful tooth you would like taken care of? How long has it been bothering you? What are your overall goals? Would you like to save it or have it removed?"

Now you have one of three basic responses: 1) Remove only; 2) Save only; or 3) I want to know the cost of either option.

Now you tailor the treatment plan to what they want. I would not show a root canal and crown cost to someone who answered #1; you are wasting your time and telling the patient you did not listen to him or her.

When talking about bigger cases, the questions just get more numerous and more detailed. Example: full/full removable dentures vs. full mouth rehab.

"I see you have a lot of concerns about your mouth and would like an overall plan. Do you mind if I ask you a few questions so that I can customize your plan to your needs?"

"Are you looking to have teeth removed, or would you like to try to save as many teeth as possible?"

"Are you okay with something that comes in and out of your mouth daily, or do you want something that stays in place permanently?"

"What are your overall goals with treatment and esthetic outcome? Which is more important to you: longevity or finances?"

And then as they answer, rephrase the answer as a question (active listening). "So if I hear you right, you would like to save teeth that are easily saved, would like to remove any that would require a root canal, and are okay with something that you would take in and out daily? I also hear that you like the idea of implants, but you are not sure they fit your budget at this time? Does that sound correct?"

Now you pretty much have the patient telling you what treatment plan they want and will accept: no root canals; yes, crowns and fillings; yes, partial or full denture; and no implants.

How would your patients react to this type of conversation? By finding out exactly what the patient wants, everyone walks away happy. And your happy patient will go off and tell everyone what a great job you did, too.

I only start talking about specific treatment after the patient has decided what they want as an overall plan, completely ignoring cost unless they bring it up. If cost is a concern, I first try to get the patient to accept the problem and decide on what they WANT. "I understand cost is a concern, and there are many ways we can help make this affordable for you. Can we first decide what outcome you want so we can then focus on ways it can fit into your budget?"

If I have to talk about money, I talk in ballpark figures. The thing to remember, though, is that we don't sell treatment, we sell solutions. I try to talk about replacement teeth and better function instead of implants. I try to talk about removal of pain instead of root canals. Try to link the treatment to what the patient's goals are. "Saving this tooth will save a little cost now, but may only last a few years. Replacing the tooth will cost a little more now, but over time, it will cost you far less. Which sounds like a better option for your current situation?"

If they want more cost details, I just work up two different treatment plans, but usually, I can get the patient to decide before any direct numbers are mentioned. When you hand the patient two plans, your chance of treatment acceptance is a lot lower because now they have to make a large decision, which most patients will not do on the spot.

Overall, if the patient decides what they want and owns that plan/idea (instead of me telling them what they need), when it comes to money, they stop caring about the actual cost and focus more on how they can pay for it. I hate the analogy, but it is like buying a car. They know it is going to cost them $10k–$40k, depending on what they want. All I try to get them to tell me is if they want the economy car, luxury car, or mid-price sedan. The discussion about finances should never be about the total cost, but about whether they want to pay in full or in payments. Obviously, that does not always work, but it does a majority of the time.

Having models of any option really helps. As I mentioned before, most patients are much better at visual concepts. I have models of hybrid dentures, locator dentures, dentures without implants, and crowns, implants, fillings, etc. Often, that helps for the patients, on the fence about options. It is amazing how many stop wanting the cheapest option when they see it in their hands. The second most common reason for not choosing the cheapest option is longevity. Dr. Gordon Christensen is well-known for his dental research into how long restorations last. Know these numbers well, and it can help significantly in getting patients all the information they need to make an informed choice. Fillings last an average of five to seven years, crowns seven to ten years, root canals ten to fifteen years, implants a lifetime, etc.

The last patient I had one day—we were the third office he had been to. He has teeth #2, 15, and 6–11 with mobility on 11. We talked about saving 6–11 (or 6–10) with crowns and a partial, doing full denture with an implant and molar support, or a hybrid denture. The only numbers I talked about were that the hybrid was $25k, the implant denture would be half that, and the crowns/partial would be less than option two. His main goal was longevity, but also having future options later and not spending everything now. He also did not want front crowns on his existing teeth. He decided on extraction of 6–11 with a lower combo partial with implant support before I ever went into detail about cost.

He left saying I was the first dentist who gave him enough information to understand what was going on, in a way he could understand, and that he finally felt confident with an overall plan. He decided the plan, and I never once told him what he SHOULD do or needed to do, I just laid out basic ballpark figures with longevity expectations and a basic understanding of the process involved.

We dentists are AMAZING at talking ourselves out of treatment. We do much better when we talk LESS and listen MORE.

It all comes down to figuring out the patient's desires and lifestyle and molding the treatment plan to fit those. If a patient comes in wanting only the cheapest option, and that is a life value to them, and dentistry is not of high value, they aren't going to be swayed into doing highly expensive periodontal surgery, regardless what you say. These are the patients telling you they would rather remove teeth than save them, or get removable dentures vs. crown/bridge. Spending a lot of time trying to convince them otherwise is just going to frustrate you and likely cause them to find another provider who listens to them.

So, with a severe perio patient, I get out of them from the first visit whether saving teeth is a priority to them or not. If not, I can cure their perio disease with extractions; then, the conversation is all about dentures and implants.

If they want to save them, we always do the SRP first and extract any hopeless teeth, advise them we will evaluate the results in one month, and see where to go from there. This gives them time to contemplate their true desires, figure out any questions they might have, and ideally bring their significant other with them. Then you tally the results with non-surgical options and discuss the pros and cons of the option they choose. They could come out of that with a plan for anything from stabilizing only, to replacements, to full mouth rehab. It all depends on their desires and needs, not mine.

The patient is in your office, so by nature, they want to treat something. What you need to figure out is what that something is. The failure comes into play when you try to talk them into treating something they don't think is important. Just last week, I saw a patient who has seen me three times in six years—comes in to have a painful tooth removed, and then disappears again until the next one hurts. I always offer to set up an exam appointment to "get ahead of the problem and stop losing teeth." He has never taken me up on the offer, and likely never will. It is not a concern or a value to him to do so; anything I try to do to change that is just going to frustrate us both. As a dentist it's unfortunate because I know I can help him, but as a business owner, it is important to realize that the production per hour that comes from keeping emergency-only patients is higher than almost any other type of patient. And I know that I can treat him as well as or better than any other dentist he has not worked with before.

People, in general, can tell if you are really there to help them or are just in it for the job or money. Many of us unconsciously portray the job only because we don't connect with the patient. We love talking about dentistry and we have a schedule to keep, so we often rush through the relationship-building conversation to get to the dentistry. What message do you think this gives to the patient?

I have had dentists ask me before, "What is the verbiage you use to help THEM decide they actually want to treat it?" In many ways, the answer is that you shouldn't. The answer is just to ask questions and LISTEN to them; then you can guide them to the best options to fit their desires.

Some patients may not want to treat the problem, and that is just fine. I am here to advise them on how to treat the problem IF they want to. This is a small difference in wording, but a huge difference in connotation and presentation. I focus far more on asking what they want and listening to what their real answers mean than I ever do trying to tell them what they want. Ironically, when you don't push, the patient often pushes themselves more than you ever could. The goal of us as providers should be, as their advocate, to be on their side always offer information, but never try to change their mind if what they want is a viable option. Very basic, palliative-only care is still a viable option if the patient desires it.

Let's look at an advanced perio scenario:

"Mr. Jones, I hear from you that you want to save as many teeth as possible. Is this correct?

Great. So you would like to start with the non-surgical approach first and remove any hopeless teeth, then re-evaluate in one month to see how things are progressing so we can come up with a long-term plan?

Great. What other questions or concerns can I help answer for you?"

Or:

"Mr. Jones, I hear from you that you are not interested in saving teeth. Is this correct?

OK, and you also only want to address the teeth that are currently causing you pain today, but you would like to schedule a full exam in two weeks once you are feeling better?

Awesome. What other questions can I help answer for you before we get started?"

Let's say you do treat the patient and see them back in a month.

"Mr. Jones, we have made some huge progress; you are looking a lot better in many areas. Can you feel the difference?

Great, so as you can see, there is still a concern in X area with 6+mm pockets. Treatment for this would require a one-hour procedure that has minimal downtime and much easier recovery than the extractions. Would you like to treat this area so you don't have to lose more teeth?

Yes? Great, we will get you scheduled with the periodontist!

No? Okay, just so I am clear, I understand that if we have to have a conversation about losing more teeth in the next year or two, you will be okay with that future outcome?

Okay, let's set you up for your three-month maintenance to help delay that as much as possible. If you would ever like to look into stopping the process of losing more teeth, I am always here to help in whatever way I can. What other questions can I help answer for you before I go?"

Remember, as a provider, our goal is to treat the patient both with best practices and by honoring their decisions and values. The key to increased treatment acceptance is providing solutions that keep both in mind.

## Chapter 15
# How to Respond to Reviews

I n this day and age, pretty much all service-related businesses are subject to online reviews. And one constant rule in life is that you cannot please everyone all the time. Being in healthcare makes this worse because we are often telling people something they don't want to hear: that something is wrong. It is almost inevitable that we upset some patients. Occasionally, it is enough to get a bad review. Learning how to handle bad reviews can help greatly with your online reputation as well as decrease the stress that comes with them.

### Direct Contact / Immediate Response
I have had several bad reviews in the past, some justified and some not. I was able to clear up many of them before they ever became a problem. An immediate response directly to the patient can go a long way to clear up any situation.

Think of it from the patient's point of view. Whether it's justified or not, they are upset about something. The main thing anyone wants when in that state is to be heard. Giving that to a patient alone can often diffuse the situation.

Along those lines, when someone wants to be heard, they usually want to be heard NOW. Again, think of this from the patient's viewpoint. Or, think of a time when you have been upset with a service provider; maybe you've been so annoyed that you've thought about leaving a review yourself. Maybe you even have gone as far as actually leaving a bad review. What pushed you to that point? How could you have felt more heard and better served?

If they took the time to write a negative review, they are upset and feel it is important to them. When you delay responding to them, all they will feel is that you do not find them important. When you respond quickly, you, at the minimum, are telling them that you recognize their concern is important to them.

## Do Not Get Defensive / Stay Professional

One of the hardest things to do when in a review situation is separate yourself from the emotion behind it all. It is only natural to get defensive and emotional when someone is seen to be attacking our office, team, or self; however, having that attitude often will make the situation worse, as the patient tends to push back by being defensive as well.

If you have ever heard the term "be the bigger person," here is where that matters.

## Find Common Ground

If it is at all possible, finding common ground is a great way to help get past the initial hurt/upset the patient is feeling. One of the most common complaints in a dental office is insurance. Dental insurance intentionally makes the process obtuse so that patients lose confidence in the dentist. Turn this back around on the insurance company and take the side of the patient.

### Redirect / Show the Patient a Path

You should always give the patient a next step to take. Most often, this is in terms of whom they need to contact next to resolve the problem, whether that is your office or another source like the insurance company.

### Highlight Any Good Parts

If the patient says anything positive about the office, thank them. It might sound odd to thank someone after they posted a bad review. However, what it does is focus the other readers towards the good instead of just the negative.

### Example In-office Review

"You are so shady; you told me my crown would be $300 and then sent me a bill later for more."

### Response

> "Mrs. Smith, I understand and share your frustration. We are on your side. We called your insurance company and talked to them directly to get a history and estimate for your case, but unfortunately, they did not honor the information they gave us. Would you like us to help you in contacting them to file a complaint for their mistake?"

You can dissect this based on what has been discussed already. First, you acknowledged the patient's concern, along with putting yourself on the same side as the patient. Second, you gave a factual history without getting defensive. Third, you went even further to focus the patient on the real problem and steps they might take in the future to resolve it. Solving these problems, small or large, in the office can go a long way to preventing them from becoming public. However, some patients will not tell you directly and just go straight to online.

## Online Review Responses

When the direct approach does not work or defuse the situation, crafting a great online response can go a long way towards taking a potentially damaging negative review and either defusing it or even turning it positive.

The first thing to remember about online responses is that your target is not the patient! Your target is every other patient in the future who will read that review and your response.

Many people out there think that not responding is a good option. I would propose a couple of reasons why that is not the case. First, the readers often have no clue who both the reviewer and responder are; they are looking for a dentist if they are reading the reviews. When they see a negative review with no response, the most likely assumptions they will make are either that the review is true or that the dentist just does not care when patients are upset. Neither are good things for you.

Second, occasionally you can get a patient to actually follow through on your suggestion to contact the office and resolve the issue. Then, often the review comes down completely. Either way is a win for the office.

The reason some people say responding is a bad idea is because if you get it wrong and misjudge the correct response, you can either make the patient more upset or make yourself look bad, thus making it worse. This is why you need to know how to respond well and avoid that trap.

## Cool Off

Before you respond to any review, you need to give yourself a little time to cool off. You never want to respond in an emotional state, because that is when you will end up saying the wrong thing. This is why being professional and brief are so important. The longer the response, the less positive effect it will have. You end up saying something that will make the patient more upset, or you end up coming across as defensive. Ideally, once you craft a response, send it to someone you know and trust to get their opinion from an outsider's perspective.

Avoid these traps:

1. Saying things like: "This is not how we routinely conduct business." This indirectly admits fault. If you are going to admit fault, do it directly and apologize. It appears far more professional.

2. Asking the reviewer a question. All you will end up doing is inciting more negative feedback.

3. Arguing with the reviewer.

4. Lying or stretching the truth.

Here is a good example from a dentist I was helping:

"We thought we had found a good family dentist that was close to home and would be a nice, clean place to have our regular checkups. My husband was first up with his appointment, but lo and behold, AFTER he was already in the chair, already had X-rays done, they conveniently told him that we were, in fact, out of network with insurance. (They had confirmed on the phone that our insurance was in-network.) You run a completely crooked business and lie to your potential new patients. You and your staff need to get their information straight when dealing with patients and insurance information. When someone calls to confirm insurance info and you say you are in-network, and then do a switcheroo ... not OK. Unacceptable."

Now, the dentist had done everything on their end right. Insurance had told them the wrong information when they first called. There were also multiple other details and circumstances involved. The first draft this dentist sent me of their response was longer than the review. I even got bored reading it, and I was the one trying to help.

Being brief is far more important than being thorough online. Remember, we live in the day of Instagram, Snapchat, Twitter, and other social media platforms that do not allow long responses. Here is one recommended response to such a review.

"We apologize your husband did not have a positive experience in our practice. We share your frustration that the insurance company gave us the wrong information when we called them, and we apologize for any misunderstanding as a result. Many of our out-of-network patients find minimal, if any, difference in cost for routine care in seeing us. Our team is happy to assist you with any further questions or concerns."

## Reassess

Now we come to the final thing that is more important than anything else when it comes to reviews. Most offices forget this step. You always want to re-assess the situation and see if there is some change you can make in the office to prevent the problem from occurring. Some reviews can be legitimate problems that are happening that you may not even know about. The more you can fix the problems, the less reason you give patients to be upset and the better your office will be overall.

"Very disappointed with their service and deceptive practices. They recommended a procedure and I was told that my dental plan would cover a majority of the procedure. I had the procedure done and then a few weeks later I received a bill for the entire procedure. I called my dental plan and they told me that the procedure was never covered. "

This was from another doctor I was helping in another state. The reviewer had a good point that the insurance person screwed up and told the patient something that ended up being incorrect. Thankfully, in this case, the patient's name was attached to the review so they could easily tie it back to the original problem. With some coaching, the dentist personally called the patient back, apologized for the error, and came to a mutually acceptable alternative with the patient. The insurance girl learned a valuable lesson about why accuracy is so important, ended up going to an insurance CE course, and is now doing very well. Due to the quick response by the dentist, the patient ended up removing the review and is still a patient at the practice. Yes, the dentist had to eat a couple hundred dollars, but their reputation is worth so much more. Overall, the practice ended up better as a result because this patient was the only one who took the time to let the dentist know about the problem. Most likely this was not the only patient who had issues.

## Avoiding Bad Reviews

Here are the most common review complaints about dentists:

1. Screwed up insurance errors
2. Billing problems
3. Rude, unprofessional
4. Failed work
5. Did not understand treatment needs before given a treatment plan

All of these can be legitimate concerns and can and should be addressed before the patient has a reason to post it online. The best way to learn is from the mistakes of others so you do not have to suffer the consequences of those mistakes yourself. For instance, why not peruse the negative reviews of some of your local competitors and make sure you're not doing anything that might cause the same responses?

## Drowning Out the Bad

Finally, we come to the last part of reviews that is actually the best part. We always have more patients who are happy than are not. The best way to remove a review that comes from a patient we just cannot please is to drown it in great reviews from all your other patients. One bad review when you only have five reviews can be a huge problem. However, one bad review when you have dozens only serves to legitimize the office. No one truly believes you can make everyone happy. When you have a perfect score, people will think you are doing something to rig the system. So when you get that one-star bad review and the patient just will not respond to any reason, then you just need to refocus and change tactics. Spend the next month drowning out that review with a dozen good ones, and it will no longer matter.

# Chapter 16
# **Associates**

M y first year, I associated with a Medicaid office while my office was being built and then while it was growing. There are multiple things that were both good and bad about the experience. Once my office got large enough, I hired a couple of short-term associates. These dentists were doing the same thing I did a few years prior: working part-time while building their office elsewhere. The greatest part about these associates was that we helped each other learn. They learned how to run a successful office, and I learned how to work with an associate. This chapter is both for associates who want to be successful, and for owners to be successful in hiring an associate.

## Compensation

I field questions all the time from associates who are asking if their contract is fair or not. The most common concerns are about percentage of work and benefits offered. The thing I am constantly trying to get both owners and associates to understand is that the individual parts don't matter nearly as much as the total compensation package. Below are a few examples to illustrate this.

## How Busy Are They?

Would you want a job that paid 40 percent of collections? If you immediately said yes, you really need to keep reading. What if I told you that same office was slow and only collected $500k, and half of that was hygiene? Your top potential earnings would be $100k.

And what if I told you instead that there was an office that was offering 30 percent collections, but it collected $1.7 million and one third of that was hygiene. Your potential earnings would be $336k—over three times as much.

Since most of us are paid for a percentage of our work, how much work we have access to do is far more important than the percentage. A massive percentage of nothing is still nothing. You will see none of this in a contract. One of the most important things to ask about as an associate (or show as an owner) is how much potential work there is to do.

## Benefits

Total compensation is what really matters at the end of the day. Corporate offices are well known for offering tons of benefits. However, how useful is that really? You really need to calculate the value of that benefit. Some dentists will mistakenly look for medical benefits, CE stipends, loan repayments, or sign-on bonuses. Would you want these things if it meant you were getting compensated far less overall?

Let's see a common example of a corporate office offering medical benefits of 50 percent of a $400 premium. Otherwise said, they would pay $200 a month, and the other $200 came out of your paycheck. This makes the medical benefit a $200 a month benefit, or $2,400 a year of total added compensation. If you increase your collections/production percentage by 1 percent, you usually end up with a higher value.

If you look at $2,500 CE reimbursement, again, a single percent increase in collections would typically get you more money overall.

So now if you look at that same corporate office and see they are paying you 25 percent plus benefits, are you still thinking that offer is better than a private practice that offers 30 percent without benefits?

## What is included in the percentage?

At my first office, I was paid 25 percent production, but nitrous and X-rays went to the office. As a new graduate, I did not realize how important that was. Working in Medicaid where every patient got X-rays and nitrous on every visit, removing nitrous and X-rays cut my production by 20–25 percent. Otherwise said, the 25 percent production was actually a 20 percent production. Now, who would get excited to be paid 20 percent without benefits? No one, I would hope. Thankfully, that job did not last long.

## Lab Bills

It is common for offices to split the cost of lab bills with the provider. I hear way too often that the "fair" way to do this is to match the percentage of compensation to the percentage of lab bill split. Meaning if you are paid 30 percent collections you pay 30 percent of lab fees. I am not sure where this idea comes from except humans like symmetry. There is no mathematical reason that this should matter at all. I hope you are seeing by now that the only thing that matters is what the math adds up to in the end. Lab bills are just another way for an office to be able to raise the percentage payment without actually adding more compensation.

Let's use an example for this. If you have an average fee of $600 for a crown and your average lab fee is $150, 25 percent of a crown is a lab fee. That means that the provider is now being charged 12.5 percent of a crown. If half of your production is from crowns, that is 6.25 percent of your total collections. So, if your 30 percent collection is dropped by the 50 percent of the lab bill, your collections percentage is really 28.1 percent. That 50 percent lab bill actually cost you a 2 percent production.

The overall point is that 28 percent of collections without lab fees is the same as 30 percent of collections with lab fees. Always remember to think about the math when you are evaluating your compensation offer. It can make a huge difference!

## Collections vs. Production

This ends up being a hot-button topic in almost any compensation discussion. I would like to remove the emotional piece of this and focus purely on facts, which are far more important if you really want to clearly evaluate compensation offers.

The first basic idea is that in general, the difference is 5 percent. Often you will see that when someone is paid 30 percent collections that will be similar to 25 percent of production. This happens for many reasons, which include collections issues of adjustments to the value to the office. It is often far easier for an office and associate to track collections because it is purely money in the bank, whereas production has a ton of adjustments from insurance write-offs, discounts, errors, etc. So when you see one offer of collections and one offer of production, remember to compare apples to apples and change that number by 5 percent.

The second thing to remember is that collections may take on average 30–60 days to come in, whether that is because of insurance or payment arrangements. This is another reason most offices that offer collections packages will pay higher. There is huge value in only paying out money that is already in the bank. This is in comparison to production, which is basically a mini-loan to the provider.

Finally, and most importantly, is how good is the office at collections? This is typically the reason why so many dentists argue against collections-based pay. You will hear emotional responses like "the provider has no control over collections." Well, that statement is wrong in many ways. True, the provider does not have direct control over office collections procedures, but they can have a huge impact on the collections efforts of the office, which I will go over in a bit.

Before we talk about that, math and history are more important than anything. If an office historically collects 85 percent of production, I completely agree that collections percentage compensation is going to be a bad thing for the associate. However, if the office has a long history of collecting 99 percent of production, collections actually ends up being a better thing for the provider and a fairer arrangement for all involved.

Now, let's talk about how the provider has an impact on collections. What happens if the provider consistently decides to do treatment before a signed treatment plan exists and before the office has collected the money? Whose fault is it now when the office cannot collect that money? Offices should have policies in place to ensure that work is only started after full collections or signed payment arrangements have been made, and the associate needs to completely follow and support these policies if they want to get paid.

Another example would be a provider who does poor-quality work or otherwise makes the patient experience an unpleasant one. When collections discrepancies come up, how likely do you think it is going to be that an unhappy patient wants to pay more money later to balance their account? Not very likely!

Finally, just like we discussed in treatment acceptance, the value the provider puts on the treatment means everything. If you put a high value on the treatment that matches the patient's goals, that patient is extremely likely to pay in full without any issues. However, if the provider happens to not match patient goals with treatment well or does not get the patient to see the value they are getting;, that patient is likely to be your collections-issue patient.

So for all associates and owners, this is why it is extremely important to give or get good training in how to communicate with patients and have great treatment planning skills so that both associate provider and owner dentist have a beneficial relationship.

# Chapter 17
# Never Stop Learning

Continuing education is important to us all. It is the way we keep updated on licensing requirements, as well as keeping up to date on changes in our professional care. There are tons of suggestions about what CE courses to take. We should all realize that we have two priorities when picking what CE to take. First, we must stay on top of the professional and technical development of our profession so that we can best serve our patients. Second, we must grow as providers and be able to offer more skills to the office, thereby growing the business. It is in the nature of any profession for most of your colleagues to be learning as well. You keep up or get left behind based on how much you decide to focus on continuing education.

Are you planning any extra training? Do you have an idea of what area to focus on? New dentists ask me a ton of questions about what to take first. My best recommendation to those of you who have recently graduated is to stick with non-clinical CE. Most dental schools in the country are going to train you well enough on clinical training, but tend to not be as strong in non-clinical training. This would include business skills, financial management skills, leadership, and communication skills. I see and have fallen for one simple trap many of us fall for. I love being a dentist, and therefore clinical CE always seems more attractive. However, there is one very important point to remember. Most clinical CEs may train you well to do something, but at some point, you still need to be able to train and lead your team as well as get the patients to understand the treatment and accept your care.

Many dentists who I would consider some of the best clinicians in the country are struggling in their offices. They have tons of clinical education and skills but have problems getting that knowledge and skill to resonate with the patient enough to get the patient to accept care and pay for it.

There are tons of CEs that we need over the years to become the best providers we can be. We need to strategically plan how we take these CEs, as there is not an unlimited amount of hours or money to take all CEs. If we take a ton of clinical courses but cannot communicate to patients well enough to get good acceptance to do those procedures, in essence, we end up wasting a lot of our training. The most successful dentists in the country are not usually the best clinical providers, but most often the most successful leaders and communicators.

I have taken hundreds of hours of CE. In my early years, I spent a lot of it on clinical CE but did not notice an overall change in my income or success. I took several clinical CE courses that were very expensive, of which many were either break-even or losses based on their cost vs. their benefit. Once I started focusing more on non-clinical education about communication and leadership, I noticed almost immediate and significant increases in not only income but also personal and patient satisfaction. What CE would have the biggest impact on your office and your career goals? What extra skills would your patients appreciate the most? Be honest in your self-assessment and judge where you will see the most return on the investment of your time.

## Consultants/Coaches

I can tell you from personal experience that consultants can be either the biggest waste of money or the absolute best investment you will ever make. The difference is between knowing what red flags to look for, and also—like with many things—what mentality you have before you start.

One of the largest red flags for a consultant or almost any company you look into working with is their commitment requirements. If someone wants you to pay in full up front or requires a long-term contract, you can be almost assured it is because they cannot keep clients happy. The only reason to force someone into long-term commitments is that you have a hard time keeping clients wanting more.

My largest waste of money to date was a consultant who only accepted clients with payment in full. He promised the most, but also asked for the most of anyone—and I have talked to dozens of consultants and companies over the years. I found out later that it was because he wanted to change how I worked so much that I couldn't imagine almost any dentists agreeing to the changes.

Another red flag is anyone trying to get you to buy into their system without pretty good details about how their process works. There is not much out there anymore that is secret with consulting. Anyone being secretive is likely hiding something. Now, don't misunderstand me, I also would not expect a consultant to spend forever giving you tips and tricks for free long-term. If you find someone who is giving you good, consistent feedback, that is helpful; personally, I would feel obligated to start paying them back for their help.

Sandy with Unlock the PPO has answered several of my specific questions over the years. She has always been a good resource, so I did try to start working with her company. The only reason I have not is because she told me that in my specific situation, she would not likely be able to provide much value.

Great, what integrity in being able to say that! This is why she gets an honorable mention here.

Expect honesty from anyone you choose to consult with and don't ignore any red flags. Communication and how you will work together, as I've mentioned before, will be tantamount in the success you will be able to achieve through their processes.

## Philosophy Differences

There are a few consultant groups that I can personally understand where they are coming from and that likely work, but I just do not agree with their methods. You are likely to find some groups that have shown good success. However, if something about how they work or what they recommend is a huge philosophical concern for you, then I would recommend just moving on. There are so many options available that you can find someone who fits you.

## Mentality

If you can navigate all the red flags, the final component in being successful with a consultant or company is YOU. Are you ready to jump in feet first and work hard to implement whatever you need to do to be successful? A simple example would be an online marketing company where you have to input the details and pictures of your office. If you don't take the time and effort to get good content, likely your success with that marketing effort is not going to be nearly as good.

With consultants and coaches, that idea is similar, just on a larger scale. When you work with someone to improve your process, it is very important to devote the needed time and effort to the process. A half-commitment on your part can only achieve partial results.

And what about your team? I can tell you from experience that if you don't also spend time learning what the team learns, you aren't likely to be on the same page as them. This is highly important for weekend trips that you take without taking the team with you. Ever notice that you come back excited with loads of new ideas, only to ultimately have a hard time getting the team on board? They did not get the same motivation you did because they did not hear the reasons and examples of why things work. If you want a CE or other informational course to be highly effective, you should include everyone who would be involved in the changes.

Another good example I always remember is the state dental conference. There are a ton of classes that we want to be taken and there is no way to get everyone to go to them all, so we give homework to each team member about their CE. We make it a point every year to get together as a team and have each person teach the others what they learned.

Very often, consultants will need information from their client as a baseline so they can see what is helping and what is not. Are you going to put effort into answering any questions, surveys, data collection, and so on that the consultant may need to help you diagnose the problems that need fixing?

And even more important, any consultant is going to need YOU as the leader of the office or as the target of change to put effort into making or leading those changes. Many times over my career, I have had successful and unsuccessful coaching. Most often, that success was dependent on my commitment to making both personal and office changes that are suggested.

# Chapter 18
# How to Motivate
# for Change

Think about some common tasks you have been doing the same way every day for years: how you dress, in what position you sleep, how you eat, the process you use to prep a crown. Now, what if someone told you that today you had to change it completely? Would you be excited or stressed? Would you be jumping for joy, or trying to find a way out?

It is human nature to resist change. This is no different for you than it is for the rest of your employees. Some dentists are blessed with amazing employees who are willing to work even harder for the same amount of pay and love doing it. The rest of us work with humans.

I cannot really pinpoint a year in which a light bulb went off when it came to managing employees, but I can say I act much differently towards my team than I used to years ago. The change and improvement I have seen over those years have been tremendous. There were a lot of stumbles along the way. See if you can relate to any.

June was a great assistant, patients loved her, and she did her job well. However, she would be consistently late every day. This problem started affecting morale in the rest of the team, since most of them are not morning people. After multiple discussions and write-ups, nothing changed, and June was eventually let go. Ever had something like this happen in your office?

Come to find out a few years later, a lot of the problem was on my end. For one, I was not asking the right questions during the interview. One of the questions I always ask now is, "Is there anything that might prevent you from showing up at 6:45 every morning?" One of my other assistants was upfront about this. She drops her son off at school and cannot be at the office until an hour after we open. In the past, I probably never would have hired her. Now, my team meets every new applicant and gets to have some input about who they bring in to help the team. This assistant was a unanimous vote, so we talked about how this concern could affect the team. They came up with a great plan: my other assistant would do her job in the morning with help from someone in the front, and the new assistant would stay later and allow others to go home more consistently on time. It was a win for the whole group, and it has worked out great for years since we hired her.

You might wonder if giving that amount of control to the team is a good idea. I wish I'd done it sooner. With some education, I let my team screen all the potential applicants now. I still maintain the ability to veto anyone should the need arise, but it hasn't yet. However, this did not happen overnight. The concept was slowly given to the team one step at a time. First, they just met each new person and gave them the tour of the office. Then, they learned to ask specific questions during that tour and to get to know the applicant (silent interview). Next, they were asked individually what their thoughts were on each applicant. Now, we do this as a group. Nowadays, I don't even have a hand in the process. Each step along the way was hard for me to give up, and it changed over several years. However, every time I did and it worked out well, there was motivation to back off more and let the team manage themselves. One of the main points to job satisfaction is feeling a sense of control and having a voice in one's job. Team interview tactics offer a great way to both get better applicants and fix problems before they arise, as well as improve team morale and job satisfaction.

## Change Is Hard

Change means new challenges and walking into the unknown. Adapting to new situations takes more effort than coasting along in a comfortable position. Is it any wonder that we don't like change? We are programmed to try to keep the status quo, and that often can be the enemy of growth and improvement. So how can we overcome our natural inclination to resist change?

First, we need to realize why it happens and acknowledge that for us and everyone around us, change is not what we naturally want. Having a plan for moving forward helps take away some of the unknown, which is another reason we resist change. The more detailed that plan is, the better able we are to make a change. Finally, we need motivation. Most often, this comes in the aspect of seeing what the future holds if we make the change. This is the main reason you will see writers or speakers give details about their successes. If you can see the example of what can happen afterward, it helps motivate you forward and overcome the challenges of breaking the status quo.

Have you ever been to a CE course and come back excited to make some change in the office, only to have your team grumble about it? They did not get to see the future you did and therefore don't have the motivation you do. Next time, take the team with you!

The same phenomenon happens with coaches and consultants as well. If they are only talking to the dentist and the rest of the team gets no vision of what the future can be, they aren't going to have the motivation to work with you. Some of the best coaches I have had came to the office to do just this. My least effective consultants were the ones the team never saw or talked to. This realization was one of many motivators for me to start coaching other dentists and going into their offices to work with the entire team directly.

Think about the last good change you made in the office. Was your team involved in seeing the vision? Think about the last change that did not work out so well. Did your team have the same vision of the goal?

## Team Buy-in

There were several years when lab cases were driving me nuts. Patients would call to complain that their case was taking too long to get seated. Labs would call with multiple questions on a case, often at inconvenient times. We even had lab cases that were months old but we could never get in touch with the patient. It was beyond frustrating that such a simple and fundamental part of treating patients was not going well.

I tried multiple ways to solve this, from write-ups to blowing up at the assistant. Rarely do these tactics ever work well, and this situation was no exception. If anything, it often made the problem worse, because now the assistant did not want to deal with it, either. I pulled multiple systems from other offices, tried the lab tracker in the management software and nothing worked.

Well, yet again, I will say that a lot of this was my fault. I was not doing well at getting the team to buy into the problem and the solution.

What finally worked was me changing my approach. You will see the system we eventually came up with in another chapter. But the system itself is not what really made it work. How I got to that system is the real magic behind it.

I decided I was going to do this differently since past attempts had failed. I am not a fan of personal insanity, so I was not going to keep trying the same tactics again. I brought both my assistants to our lab area, and we sat down and had a team meeting. I laid out the concerns from both me and the patients, with several examples of how it was affecting the office flow. They nodded along because they saw it all too. Then I asked them how we could change this. The magic happened when I stopped talking. They started coming up with ideas themselves. I just kept asking questions along the way until they had come up with a system to fix all the problems we were having with lab cases.

Within a couple weeks, everything was fixed. Patients stopped complaining, the old cases were delivered or accounted for and archived, and I stopped having to worry about them anymore. It was heaven! I had given the assistants two important things: validation of their worth in the office, and the ability to feel like they had a say in how their work life was organized. Yes, I controlled a lot of it based on when and how I asked the questions. The process, though, was what allowed a major change to occur without nearly as much headache. I learned that leaders get far more done when they inspire change. I listened more and asked questions instead of demanding and dictating. You will be pleasantly surprised what a difference it can make!

Do you inspire change in your team, or do you struggle? In what ways can you think of how this might impact a current issue in your office?

## Become a Leader

Leaders are motivators instead of dictators. Excellent leaders can draw out the potential in others and inspire them to change and improve. Often, they ask more questions and listen instead of just telling people how to do something. They can get others to see a vision instead of just a process. Are you a natural leader? Most people aren't, but we can all learn to do better!

Let's start with some examples of poor leadership, since they are more common and relatable.

## Fair

Have you ever worked in an office where some employees were treated differently than others? One employee was given some favoritism, and it created a rift in the team dynamic. Imagine if you were the employee who was left out; how would you feel? How about the employee who was always favored; do you think they might come to believe they are somehow better than their coworkers and not be able to work as a team with them? This dynamic is common in many offices and often comes about with poor leadership. I have been unintentionally guilty of this in the past; have you? Leaders inspire harmony and balance within the group and are seen being fair with everyone they encounter.

## Accountability and Follow Through

This is the one I have suffered from the most. There are multiple examples in which I started a program, new procedure, or different process and did not hold others and myself accountable enough to see it through to the end. I picked up a new TMJ therapy skill but did not follow through on the recording and marketing of it. Therefore, I did not end up doing enough of it to solidify the skill, and eventually I stopped talking about it to patients. Ultimately, it was a waste of money and effort because of this, and the equipment is now collecting dust in my office. Is there any equipment in your office that is collecting dust for similar reasons?

If you follow US politics much, you know healthcare is a common point of concern for many Americans. Do you know that congress members are exempt from the new healthcare laws that they enacted? Do you believe this is fair, or does it make you have less respect for those who would enact a federal law that excludes the lawmaker? Our offices are no different. I have been guilty of changing processes in the office and then not holding myself just as accountable as the rest of my team. When we tell our team to do something we are not willing to do ourselves, we often lose the respect of our team. Excellent leaders know that they must hold themselves to a higher standard than those they lead. We also must keep track of the changes we want to happen and make sure our team is following through.

Think about this. You enact a change in the process the team follows in how they talk to patients. Change is hard, and the status quo is easy. If you did not follow up and ask your team regularly how that change is going, what do you think might happen? Will they keep doing what is hard? Or will they revert to what is easy and known? Leaders understand that habits are hard to form and easy to break. They know they must hold others accountable to the new changes and follow up regularly until those changes become habits.

## Emotions and Stability

Do you know of a dentist who gets overly emotional and throws instruments across the room or at their assistants? How about one who yells at their team and berates them in front of patients or other team members? If you ask most assistants who have worked in several offices, you will notice it is all too common a story. And the story does not come with a feeling of respect towards the dentist involved.

There is a time and place for emotions, and we are all human and may occasionally have a bad day. The key is to make sure those days are so rare that the team accepts the fact that you are still human and accepts your apology when they happen. Leaders strive to be the balance in the office. They help others by being the example of how to act and treat others. Leaders only build people up in public, and never knock them down. When they fail, leaders are quick to admit fault and apologize for their mistakes.

Recently, I had a negative review from a patient about the office and our hygiene department. This was one of our only negative reviews in over a year. I take all comments and reviews seriously, so I investigated it. I pulled data from the last year about patients who had started scaling and root planning but never returned. One of my hygienists had a higher number of patients who did not return. So, I brought her in and talked to her about the concern. She apologized for any issues and asked if she could look more into it. She came back the next day with more information. Yes, she had more patients who did not come back after initial SRP, but she also treated more than double any other hygienist number of SRPs. With the expanded data, it showed she had the highest percentage of patients who returned for maintenance. Suffice to say, that was a major error on my part.

I handled the conversation correctly but did not investigate the data enough to come to the best conclusion. Having supporting information is so important when you are looking at trends to try to change them. When you are wrong, you can lose respect from those around you. Leaders learn to look at the bigger picture, lead from solid information, and double-check their sources.

## Learn How to Motivate Change

This negative review also sparked a change I was planning on doing for a while. In 2018, Google changed their algorithm for reviews, and many dentists lost half or more of their online reviews. As discussed in the chapter on reviews, burying bad reviews with good ones is one of the best ways to combat people who are unreasonable and lash out online.

I had tried several things over the years to get my team focused on online review generation. I complained that they weren't asking enough. I lashed out whenever we got a bad review and tried to make sweeping changes off of one experience. I bought into several programs that were supposed to simplify and automate the process. I hope you can guess by now that none of these tactics worked. These are not the tactics of a good leader.

By now, I had learned my lesson and decided to try something different. I had a team meeting and discussed the concern with them as a group. Marketing is often about reviews, and in over nine years, we had only achieved a total of eighty reviews between Google and Facebook, which had just been cut in half by the new changes. I got a lot of interesting responses in that meeting.

"Happy patients will leave reviews naturally. It sounds desperate to ask for reviews."

So I asked: Do we have a lot of patients who are happy when they leave? Do we have patients and their family and friends that we have seen for years? Of course we do! So, if we have treated a few thousand patients over a nine-year period and only have eighty reviews (now forty) to show for it, do patients leave reviews naturally? Of course, they don't; people have busy lives and rarely is the dentist at the top of their list. If some offices are getting in one year what we're getting in nine years, does it stand to reason that they are asking for reviews? Do they sound desperate or look great with those glowing patient responses?

"The doctor does not ask for reviews. We don't have time during the day to do this as well. We aren't comfortable asking. Who should be asking? We don't know which patients to ask", etc.

All the concerns and questions that came up were good ones in the sense that they highlighted the true problem. Consciously asking for reviews was a big change. Change is hard. The unknown is scary. The team was basically saying they needed more information and a process to follow so they can be more comfortable with this new change.

Now, the old me would have dictated the process, given all the answers, and expected the team to agree with me. Instead, what worked even better took far less effort on my part. By now my team is very used to being given a task, running with it, and developing their own process. I just set the goal, and a bonus to reach that goal each month. Actually, I set three goals of increasing amounts, each one paying them a larger bonus per review if they got more each month. However, they would only earn the bonus money for three months, so if they did not push themselves fast enough, they would lose out on the potential extra pay. Once I saw their eyes light up and the wheels start turning, I walked away and let them handle the rest. By the end of the day, my assistant came to me and told me the software for review requests was not working. None of them had really paid attention to it before because they weren't really using it. Magic happened after that, and reviews started coming in: usually one or two a day.

The plan worked. My team had figured out solutions to their own hurdles, and it was working even better than if I had tried to micromanage the process myself. Now, I offer a point of caution to you. If this is one of the first times you are allowing your team to manage themselves, you are likely to need to give them more input to get them going. Just like it takes practice and experience to become a great dentist or a great leader, it will take time for your team to get to the point where they are self-managed and you can give a vision and walk away. However, this is the ultimate goal to shoot for: a team that manages itself and often works better with less input from you.

Once the three months are up, the team will no longer be bonused on reviews. However, the fact remains that they can achieve those results, and they will become expected in the future. They will have proven to themselves that all their concerns that stopped them from doing it in the first place were either invalid or had solutions. This way, you incentivize quick and better results, but don't have to keep paying for those results forever. Once you develop the habit, it will naturally keep going.

Are there any changes in the office that you want to make and could apply these ideas to? What would it mean for you and the office to make that change with less hassle?

## Implementing Change

Think about a large patient treatment case. If you have to do some form of full-mouth rehab, what are the steps involved? You are going to want some diagnostic data, maybe some wax-up or preliminary model, potentially a trial provisional, the final restoration, and then maintenance. It might take months to a year to get all that done correctly. What would happen if someone told you that you had to do all that in a month? Would you feel confident about the final outcome?

Implementing large or multiple changes is not much different. You will want the data to make the correct changes. You will want a plan and model of how to get the change you want. And you will need maintenance to keep up the change you have created.

I have made many, many changes since I opened, as you will notice. Some attempts have been far more successful than others. The longer I go and the more I learn, the more often these changes become successes. Potential changes and ideas will come from many sources, from CE courses, colleagues, seminars, books, mentors, consultants, etc. My least successful attempts happened almost always: when I tried to change too much at once. Remember that change is hard and takes effort. Change also requires planning, accountability, a vision, and follow-through. When you try to change too much at once, you will burn out yourself or your team and destroy the very progress and motivation you are trying to create.

The most effective way to make change is by taking small steps. I hope you have gleaned several tips from my journey that you want to implement. My suggestion to you is to prioritize those changes and make them at a reasonable pace. We are working with team members who are still human. In general, I have found that people can handle one big change or a couple of small changes at a time without burnout. We also take anywhere from one to three months for that to become habit enough to repeat without thinking, depending on the size of the desired change. Keep this in mind.

My suggestion is to write down all the changes you want to make or investigate. By writing them down, you are far more likely to follow through. Next, prioritize that list. You might want to go by ease of the change, or things that might make the biggest bang quickly. When you have small successes, it will help drive you and your team forward to larger ones. Finally, evaluate your list and be realistic about what you can accomplish and make a habit of in each period of time. If you have a team that is ready, you can bring them into the loop of changes and enlist their help in creating this master list. Once you have your plan, all you need to do is follow through with the treatment based on the plan.

Always keep in mind that as a leader, you need to be the example of the change you want to see in those around you.

Now, if you have not done this before, it may be a daunting task. Seeking outside help can be of huge benefit, whether it comes from a colleague, mentor, or coach. Having outside help can be huge in keeping you grounded in what can be accomplished in a given time, as well as giving you someone to help hold you accountable and keep you moving forward. It can also help give your team third party validation that the changes you want to make can work

What changes do you want to make in your office or life? Do you have someone who can help you with implementation? Once you make the change, what does success look like to you?

# Chapter 19
# Defining Success

As they say, before one can achieve success, one must define success.

Living in America, the common definition of success is often based on your income. I would challenge that notion and say that success is not that narrow of a focus. Think about why you want money. Of course, money makes the world go around. Everything is purchased with money. However, does the physical (or these days electronic) money by itself make you happy? Or is it more what the money brings you that makes you happy? Small amounts of money can buy you food. Large amounts of money buy cars, houses, luxuries, etc. So what do all of those have in common? Freedom to choose. Think about it, what makes you happier and more fulfilled? Was it the food itself, or the idea that you could choose a steak over the hamburger and not care about the cost?

What is your definition of success? What kind of life do you want to lead?

I live near Plano, a large city north of Dallas. It is a beautiful area with lots of large homes. However, there is a very common problem there. People often are house-rich and cash-poor. They live in large homes that most people would think are amazing, but they are so poor because of their house that they cannot afford to do anything. I doubt most of them are truly happy with their circumstances when they have to scrimp their budget to actually live. What is the point of a large house if your life is empty?

Now think about your dental office. The offices that make less than average collections with high overhead and minimal growth aren't your typical definition of success. Often, we see with dentists here who are worried about saving money on every tiny expense, are feeling overworked and underpaid, and usually aren't thrilled with their situation. On the extreme end, these are the doctors who often ask, "Why did I become a doctor in the first place?"

Let's look at the other extreme: the offices that have huge collections, small overhead, and good growth. The doctor tends to feel fulfilled and genuinely happy about their situation, right?

It's time to think about some of the other aspects, which can be as important if not more so. A few years ago, I had that crazy busy office. Collections were very high, overhead was decent, and growth was going great. However, I had a ton of stress, was bringing work home frequently, and felt constrained by the office. Taking time off for breaks or even a vacation was extremely tough, and every time, I felt like the office was suffering while I was away. Have you ever felt constrained by the office?

As a contrast to that, a good friend of mine in Nevada runs an office that collects half of what I do. His overhead is minimal, his stress is zero, he works three days a week, and he takes two months of vacation every year. He makes enough money to be happy but also has the flexibility of time to do almost whatever he wants. Which would you prefer?

The key to success is finding the balance between income and flexibility that gives you the freedom most of us are really seeking. For each person, this combination is slightly different depending on our specific goals and life. Running a successful business is about being able to mold the business to fit your goals in both time and income and stay below your stress threshold. So next time you wonder, "Am I successful?" I would suggest that instead of comparing yourself to another office, remember to look at the bigger picture and see if you are getting both financial freedom as well as freedom of time that fits your life. If you aren't, then why not take the next steps towards that goal?

# Epilogue

My goal in writing this book was to help others avoid similar mistakes and learn ways to grow professionally. I hope I was able to provide you with some cautions in what to avoid so you do not make the same mistakes I did. If some of the mistakes I made resonate with you for being in the same boat, I hope that you found some inspiration that there is a brighter path ahead.

There are so many factors that are affecting dentists today, from insurance to corporate involvement. Dentistry is no longer what it was fifty or even twenty years ago. In the past, we had no true competition or drive to force us to run an efficient business. The changes we see now in the industry will continue to force us to adapt; however, I still believe that opportunity exists to run a profitable private practice dental office. Change can be hard, but it does not have to be a negative influence. We provide a much-needed service to our community, and with some effort and knowledge, we can achieve a satisfying and successful life balance.

My question to you now is: what are you going to do next? Will you make an effort to make a positive change in your life and office? I challenge you to make that effort. Whether that is making a few small tweaks or planning out lots of change, improvement looks different for everyone. Success is dependent on your goals. Money usually buys you freedom; just make sure you aren't losing freedom to earn the money. What change in your life has the potential to increase your freedom?

Seek out what you need to take that next step. If you aren't sure what to do next or just want help, I welcome you to contact me and ask. There is no limit to the success you can achieve, and it all starts with one step.

# About the Author

Dr. Travis Campbell is a full-time practicing dentist. He started his practice from scratch after graduating from Baylor College of Dentistry (2009) and has grown this single dentist practice to be in the top 1% in the country. Having made the typical mistakes as a new business owner, he has worked diligently to learn how to become a highly capable business owner. He has a passion for helping others avoid the typical dental business pitfalls and become highly successful business owners, "CEOs" and team builders in addition to being Doctors. As a result, Dr. Campbell has become well known for his knowledge/experience in dental business management and efficiency. He is an author, speaker at dental seminars, a contributor of various on-line dental communities and a dental coach/consultant.

If you would like more information or have a question for Dr. Campbell, please visit PracticeWhisper.com to learn more or to contact him directly.